YOU'RE DOING GREAT!

ALSO BY TOM PAPA

Your Dad Stole My Rake:
And Other Family Dilemmas

YOU'RE DOING GREAT!

AND OTHER REASONS TO STAY ALIVE

TOM PAPA

ST. MARTIN'S
PRESS
NEW YORK

For Cynthia

First published in the United States by St. Martin's Press,
an imprint of St. Martin's Publishing Group

YOU'RE DOING GREAT! Copyright © 2020 by Tom Papa. All rights reserved. Printed in
the United States of America. For information, address St. Martin's Publishing Group,
120 Broadway, New York, NY 10271.

www.stmartins.com

Designed by Steven Seighman

Library of Congress Cataloging-in-Publication Data

Names: Papa, Tom, author.
Title: You're doing great! : and other reasons to stay alive / Tom Papa.
Description: First edition. | New York : St. Martin's Press, 2020.
Identifiers: LCCN 2019054417 | ISBN 9781250240392 (hardcover) |
    ISBN 9781250240408 (ebook)
Subjects: LCSH: American wit and humor. | Conduct of life—Humor. |
    United States—Civilization—21st century—Humor.
Classification: LCC PN6165 .P37 2020 | DDC 818/.602—dc23
LC record available at https://lccn.loc.gov/2019054417

Our books may be purchased in bulk for promotional, educational, or business
use. Please contact your local bookseller or the Macmillan Corporate and
Premium Sales Department at 1-800-221-7945, extension 5442, or by email at
MacmillanSpecialMarkets@macmillan.com.

First Edition: May 2020

10 9 8 7 6 5 4 3 2 1

CONTENTS

INTRODUCTION

Greetings!

It's good to see you again. I would like to start by thanking you for liking my first book enough, or at least buying enough of them, that my publisher called and asked if I would write another. This made me very happy, because not only do I like writing them but also it stops me from spending all my time baking bread, drinking red wine, and looking for cheeses. Not that I stopped any of those things to write this book, but it's good to have something else to do.

I also knew exactly what I wanted to write about.

While it was really fun meeting everybody at my book events and shows over the past year, I have to admit that I'm a little worried about you. You seem stressed, overworked, and, frankly, a little mixed up.

Everyone seems to be fighting this overwhelming feeling that things are getting worse, that we should be doing more, and that we're not good enough. People are doing yoga at the airports, taking antidepressants by the handful, and drinking record amounts of alcohol, all in an attempt to not completely lose it.

Well, I'm here to tell you that it's time to calm down and realize that you're doing great! You really are. I see how hard you work and how much you care and I'm telling you, you're doing great.

We are the first human beings to be inundated, twenty-four hours a day, with news, images, and ideas of all kinds devised by forces beyond our control, and it's messing with our heads. They seep into our lives and are warping our perception of the world.

So while we aren't dealing with a major war, we are at war for the control of our own thoughts. So let's recalibrate, turn off the devices, and open our eyes to a better reality. You're doing great!

I'll go one better—you're peaking right now. Seriously, if you have time in your life to sit and read this silly book, it's not going to get much better. In the not-too-distant future people are going to ask you to go somewhere and you'll have one question: "Are there stairs?" And if there are, you're not going. These are the good times.

Life isn't perfect. There have always been problems and there always will be. You can engage politically, you can fight for the things that you believe in, you can work really, really hard, but you shouldn't lose track of the fact that while we're doing all that, life is flying by at lightning-fast speed. We live in an amazing time filled with airplanes, scooters, and peanut-butter cups. We have air conditioning, blenders, and martini shakers. It's time to refocus, enjoy it all, and realize that you're doing great.

Remember the fable about the ants and the grasshopper? All summer long the ants were working away preparing for the coming winter while the grasshopper was screwing around swimming and making out in the grass. Well, at the end of that story, winter takes hold and the ants all laugh from inside their warm homes as the grasshopper is outside freezing his unprepared hoppers off.

This tale isn't entirely accurate.

There's nothing wrong with being a grasshopper, just don't be an *arrogant* grasshopper. Do your work, of course, but keep in mind that life is to be lived and there's nothing wrong with a dip in the pool once in a while. If you want to slow down, take the day off, and make love to another grasshopper, it's okay to call in sick, put on a top hat, and have some fun.

Because the truth is, the end of the story for the ants and the grasshopper is exactly the same. But only one is going to die with a smile on their face.

So enjoy this book, enjoy some cheese, and better yet, enjoy your life.

HAVE YOU EVER SAT DOWN TO READ A BOOK AND SPENT THE FIRST TEN MINUTES TRYING TO FIND A COMFORTABLE READING POSITION AND WHEN YOU FINALLY DID YOU FELL ASLEEP? I HAVE…

YOU DON'T HAVE TO LIVE YOUR BEST LIFE

How much more do we have to do?!

We're all working really hard. We're doing stuff. We're recycling. We're letting people merge. We're reading books and doing our best. So why isn't it enough? Why do we all think that we should be doing more or at least stop being such total losers?

I blame social media, which is something I like to blame for almost everything lately, but in this case I think I'm accurate. Having a window to the entire world in the palm of our hand has created an unrealistic level of high expectations. Every time I pick it up I'm confronted with the same questions: "Are you killing it today?" "Are you 100 percent maxed out all the time?" "Are you living your best life?"

No. No, I'm not. I'm not doing any of those things. Because that's not normal! I don't care what The Rock's Instagram says, it's not normal.

You know what's normal? How you feel right now, in your funny little gassy body. A little light-headed, kind of achy, worried about your bills, and worried about that thing you found on your ass. That's normal. And it's exhausting.

That's normal, too. Being tired all the time, which I know you are, is expected.

Life is exhausting. You don't need a 5-Hour Energy drink, you need to lie down once in a while.

And yet we beat ourselves up about it all the time. Every day I hear my friends complaining, "I don't know what's wrong with me. Every day around two o'clock in the afternoon, I get sooo tired. What's wrong with me?"

There's nothing wrong with you. You woke up in the dark, went off to a job you don't enjoy, worked for five hours, ate a twenty-minute lunch, and now you need a nap and they won't let you. So you're forced to hide from your coworkers in the bathroom stall with your feet up, as you close your eyes for thirty seconds trying to get through the day without falling over.

This is hard. It's hard being a person. You have to give yourself a break. Just the physical maintenance of you every day is endless. The nonstop brushing, cleaning, and wiping, hopefully every day, is enough to drive anybody mad. It's like you are your own pet, and not everybody takes good care of their pet. You see a lot of people out there eating out of the garbage with their hair all matted and their collar missing.

Just the list of stuff you have to do to get out of the house is never ending. I saw a businessman in New York walking down Sixth Avenue. He was perfectly thought out and put together. Suit, tie, leather shoes that matched his briefcase. He had perfect teeth, glasses, and not a hair out of place. Only his fly was open and one of his testicles was sticking out!

I understood. He did everything on the list and just forgot that one item. There he was, on his way to a meeting or more likely on his way back from a meeting. That's the thing about being an adult—nobody helps you. Nobody cares. They probably looked him right in the eye in that meeting and thought, "I'm not telling him, I've got my own problems. I think I might be wearing my wife's underwear today, I don't know what the hell happened this morning."

His wife probably kissed him goodbye at the door, thinking, "What a jackass. Oh well, he'll figure it out. If I have to see it, so should everybody else. It wouldn't hurt to get a little sun on that guy once in a while anyway."

Nobody cares. We're totally alone. Even the people closest to us get only so close. We're really the only ones looking out for us. You have to give yourself little pep talks all day long, like a crazy person, because you're the only one who really cares about you.

"I've got my wallet, I've got my cell phone, now where are my keys, where are my keys, here they are. Okay. It's going to be a great day!"

The only difference between you and a crazy person is that they say it out loud on a busy street.

It's hard to keep it all together, and that's why we have to cut ourselves some slack. Just because you have nothing exciting to post on social media doesn't mean that you don't have anything going on. You always have a lot going on. Your life is enormous and meaningful, and documenting every minute of it will not make it more so.

And you don't have to be happy all the time. You really don't. Here's a little secret for you: No one is happy all the time. Clowns run around pretending they are but then end up psychotic and never get invited to dinner parties.

The reality is, we get little moments of happy in a sea of misery. Human beings are uncomfortable most of the time and that's how life works. We're not always going to be happy, and we're not always going to fit in. Life is a pair of skinny jeans and you are a big, fat ass.

But because of social media we think we're lacking.

I read a report that people are becoming clinically depressed because they're looking at other people's lives and think that their life pales in comparison.

Calm down.

First of all, no one has a great life. No one. They're posting pictures of the best moments in their life, with a filter, to make you feel shitty about yours. It's a lie. Social media is like a photo album with all the bad parts taken out.

Everyone is posting gorgeous, well-lit pictures of their vacations, smiling in front of the Eiffel Tower or on a gondola in Italy. But notice that no one posts pictures of themselves stuck at baggage claim or trapped in the hotel for a week because the husband's got diarrhea from a French tart he shouldn't have eaten. But that's happening, too, trust me.

Whenever I see couples posting about how in love they are, I know they're in trouble. Anything with more than two photos and seven love emojis and you can bet that someone has screwed up. I mean, who are they doing it for? It's not for us, we don't care. It's a weird level of public affection that makes Tom Cruise jumping on Oprah's couch, screaming about how in love he was, seem normal.

But we all get caught up in it. You see people with money and fame and it's easy to think, "What's wrong with my life? Why don't I live like that?" But the truth is, you don't want that. That's an illusion.

Remember when everyone was in awe of Brad Pitt and Angelina Jolie? They were the perfect couple, living the perfect celebrity life that we were all supposed to emulate. But look at that life. You don't want that. Their marriage is over, they're fighting over the children, it's rough stuff. But that was arrogance. You can't put two perfect people in the same marriage and think it's going to work. That's never going to work. You have too many options.

If you want your marriage to last, you need a little funny looking in it. You need to look across the table and think, "Where are you going to go?" When you're young and stupid you think you want a supermodel. No, you moron. You don't want some beautiful woman asking to be taken to Europe. You want a girl with a crooked eye asking if you have jumper cables. That's your girl. She's a keeper.

A simple life is what wins in this world. A simple life. This is a life: You run out of toothpaste. You need more toothpaste. You tell yourself that for a week and a half. You're stepping on it, squeezing it, pushing through the hole from the inside just to get a little on your brush so you don't feel like a monster out in the world. When you finally remember to stop at CVS on your way home, and you slide that fresh tube out of that long box, you feel like a winner. You really feel like you did something.

Well, guess what? You did! You're a champ and that's a life. A really great life.

And you don't have to post a thing about it.

HAVE YOU EVER GONE TO A FRIEND'S HOUSE, EATEN A SNACK OFF THE COUNTER, AND REALIZED THAT YOU JUST ATE THEIR DOG FOOD? I HAVE . . .

WE ARE FAN PEOPLE

It's important in life to learn to go without. It's a lesson that is best learned young as it will help you deal with a complicated and challenging life. You can learn this lesson many ways, but the easiest method is to have lived with my father.

My father didn't believe in air conditioning, which means he didn't want to pay for air conditioning, despite the fact that we lived in New Jersey, which is a punch line for a lot of reasons, but in the summer months it's mainly because of the humidity. The air grows thicker than a wet army blanket and holds you down like a bully smothering you with his ass. New Jersey summer air is the reason air conditioning was invented, but honestly we knew nothing about it. We didn't know it existed. How could we have? My father had cut us off from the civilized world like we were an ancient tribe in the Congo.

We were like the Yanomami tribe that I learned about in high school. The Yanomami were an isolated tribe in South America that never came in contact with the modern world, so they operated in their own reality. The men wore a stick around their penis as pants and a headband made of grass. Their idea of jewelry was poking and twisting their skin into blisters. Much like the people of the Yanomami tribe, we were ignorant of the ways of the modern world. I thought it was normal when every summer I would lie on the unfinished basement floor with my sisters as we pretended that we were slabs of beef in a meat locker. A lot of kids pretended they were Rocky. We pretended we were the meat.

Summer always seemed to catch my father by surprise. It was as if he had no idea during the spring that it would eventually get hotter. It wasn't until one of those hot July nights when the trees started to sag and the mosquitoes were too hot to fly that he realized summer was here. It was time to gather the Fans.

The Fans were a series of cockeyed contraptions that he collected throughout the years from other men who lived by the fan. In his mind there were "Air-Conditioner People" and "Fan People." We were Fan People. Air-Conditioner People wore ascots and leather loafers and ate clams casino served out of poor people's cupped hands. They "summered" in the Hamptons and sailed around in yachts that poor people rowed. They were the type of people who saw a phone next to the toilet in a hotel bathroom and weren't surprised.

Fan People lived by the earth. They barely used electricity and bought their cars used and never traded them in as long as there was a chance they could fix it themselves. They didn't do crazy things like eat in restaurants and buy name-brand potato chips. They bought their home furnishings at garage sales and flea markets or, better yet, found them at the dump.

My father loved going to the dump. He made it a weekend activity for us. Something we could be proud of. I'd come back to school and hear how kids went to an amusement park or the beach. The teacher would ask what I did and I would say proudly,

"I went to the dump!" I was unaware that other families didn't consider that a fun activity.

Going to the dump meant gathering up all the garbage that the garbageman wouldn't take. Some of it was too big to fit in the can. Some of it was made of dangerous materials that couldn't go to the landfill. Some of it my father simply held off to the side just for the opportunity of making a visit to the dump.

"They probably won't take this box of magazines, better start a pile for the dump," he'd say while fighting back a smile.

We didn't have a truck. We never had a truck. We lived in New Jersey and drove around in sedans. We were Fan People who drove sedans that are about as exciting as a pair of "slacks."

I never liked my father's cars. They were American made from the 1970s and 1980s, which in car culture are known as "the shit years." They had no shocks, so while my father was driving in one direction we would sway and bob in the other like a boat lost at sea.

They were the kinds of sedans that had carpet on the walls and cloth on the ceiling to create the feeling of a luxurious living room. The rug would get food stuck in it and the cloth would eventually detach from the ceiling and fall down around us, making it feel like we were driving through a theater curtain.

The main reason my father loved his sedan was because it had a giant American-size trunk that was perfect for the dump. We'd pack that Oldsmobile with stacks of newspapers, old *National Geographic* issues, bottles, and a lot of cans—Paint cans, soup cans, oil cans, even old gas cans with some gas still in them.

When the trunk was full he'd start filling up the back seat. A lot of times he'd have to put the windows down so the long stuff could stick out the sides, and it was my job to sit in the passenger seat facing backward so I could stop things like fireplace screens or roof shingles from flying out on the turns. I felt important whenever he gave me a job to do, but a job stopping stuff from flying out into traffic seemed extra important. I'd get in position as he started her up and backed slowly out of the driveway like a tugboat leaving the dock.

"Ooh, boy, this is some load today," he'd say with pride. I'd reach in for a better grip.

The dump was really a giant trash compactor that sat in the back parking lot of the public swimming pool. It was a big beast of a machine that was fenced except for the opening where a man sat in a folding chair waiting for people to come. It was his job to decide what could be thrown in the compactor and what could not.

To a lot of people he was an anonymous public worker, but my father was on a first-name basis with him. My father enjoyed this honor the same way some people like knowing the maître d' or the bartender at the local bar.

"Well, well, look what the cat dragged in."

"Got some crap for you, Carl," my father would say.

"Got some crap for you, too."

"Any fans?"

"Maybe," he'd tease with a chuckle.

My father loved hearing this. This meant that off to the side there was some stuff that was spared the compactor because it just might be worth saving. We got a lot of our appliances this way. Over the years my father accumulated six or seven toasters, a waffle iron, even an "extra" refrigerator that never worked but stayed in our garage for decades.

And hundreds of fans.

Carl knew to hide those special for my father. Rusty ones. Big ones. Some that looked like boat propellers. Some from the early days of oscillation. There were heavy ones made out of steel with the name of a true American company from Pittsburgh or Cleveland patriotically welded to the front. These weren't the plastic fans that you find in college dorm rooms today. These were fans that were used to cool down hardworking, Depression-era patriots. These were for Fan People.

And every July when we reached peak sweat he'd drag them out of the basement, set them up around the house, and plug them all in. They took so much power that the lights in the entire house would flicker as they came to life.

I'm not saying they weren't powerful. They were very powerful. The way a wind turbine or jet engine is powerful. Some would spin with a ferociousness that could easily cut off all your fingers. But they were no match for New Jersey humidity. All this army of fans could do was push the hot, suffocating air around the room and on top of the children.

I didn't know much, but I knew there had to be a better way. It didn't make sense to live like this. And soon we found out that we didn't have to.

It was after a particularly hot night, one of those nights when it's so hot that you sweat through your sheets. When it's so hot that the dog tries to open the refrigerator with his tongue. When it's so hot that you can't sleep so you just stare out the window and pray the sun doesn't return and make it even hotter.

My sister Kristin and I were splitting a piece of ice at the kitchen table when our sister Jen came back from a sleepover at her friend's house. While we were sweaty and defeated, she looked refreshed and renewed, as if she had slept for a week straight. She had a look on her face that said she had seen the future.

"Where were you?" Kristin asked.

"I was at Debbie's house," Jen responded.

"Why are you so happy?" I asked.

"It was so nice there."

"Nice? It was the hottest night of the year!" stammered Kristin.

"Was it? I hadn't noticed. I was sleeping in *air conditioning*."

We didn't know it, but that was the moment we lost her. Our sister, our companion through many long, horrible summers as Fan People, had been to the other side. She escaped the Congo by station wagon and was introduced to Air-Conditioner People.

"What the hell is air conditioning?" Kristin demanded to know.

"It's what rich people use to cool off their homes. You wouldn't understand," she said as she made herself an iced tea. She never made iced tea before. None of us had. Who was this person?

Anger combined with sweat and filled our eyes. We marched into the TV room where my father was aiming a fan at my poor mother, who looked like a woman from the late 1800s who had fainted on one of those fainting couches.

"We need air conditioning!" we yelled.

My father turned and slowly wiped off his brow. "What did you say to me?"

"We heard all about it. Jen was at Debbie's and she's been back for an hour and she's still not sweating."

My mother tried to lift her head off the couch pillow. "Who said what to Debbie, now?"

"Lie down, Mother."

My father stormed out of the room and turned up the fans. It didn't make us any cooler, but he could no longer hear our complaints.

My sister was banned from Debbie's house, but the secret was out. We started noticing that every place we went was colder than our home. Suddenly supermarkets, movie theaters, and ice-cream shops took on an air of wealthy elegance. We didn't just notice the cold, we smelled the money.

Later in the summer, my father, feeling the pressure, gathered us all together in the hallway and announced that he was about to turn on the greatest invention of all time. We were excited. Had the big guy sprung for air conditioning? Were we about to be cooled off without having to lie on the basement concrete? Were we rich?

"I've installed—an attic fan!"

While I was disappointed, I had to admire his dedication. Refusing to change teams, he'd decided to go in even harder on the fans. I'm not sure where he'd heard of it. I'm not sure what it cost. But he'd purchased what must have been to him the ultimate achievement for a Fan People family.

This is a giant fan, so big that in order for it to be installed they have to cut a hole through the peak of the house. A slatted door replaced the attic entrance, where normally the ladder comes down, and when a switch was flipped in the hallway closet, air is pulled from the hot house, into the attic, and out through the fan.

"Is everybody ready?"

We scowled.

He turned it on. The slats opened. He smiled. It was working. A giant hum roared through the house. And then all at once the air was sucked out of the bedrooms, slamming all the doors shut.

"Get to your doors," he yelled. "Use something to wedge them open."

He was screaming like a captain on a ship in the middle of a typhoon. We pushed against the wind to our bedrooms as he cranked it higher. Kristin was pushed across the floor in her nightgown like a leaf.

"Use a shoe or a chair. Anything," he screamed.

We all propped open our doors and it worked. It actually worked. There was an amazing breeze racing through the house. And it was cooling us off. It really was.

"Fuck Debbie's house," Kristin said.

We were Fan People. And we were proud. And on this night, we had won. We defeated those high bills that the Air-Conditioner People didn't even open. We slept well, with a cold breeze flowing over all of us. We thought the war was over. We were fools.

The humidity returned, and the attic fan, like all fans, was no match. It was now sucking humid air from all over the metropolitan area through the house like a tropical storm. We were hot. We were sweaty. We had lost. And if there was any doubt that we were Fan People, we found my father standing in the middle of the kitchen in nothing but his underwear, with a square metal fan, atop a stool, aimed at his sweating belly.

My mother stood in the doorway with her children behind her, all of us looking like we had just drifted up on shore like Cuban refugees. She walked over, looked him in the eye, and unplugged it. The fan slowly came to a stop.

"But we're Fan People," my father muttered.

"We were," she said. "But not anymore."

He might have cried. There was too much sweat on his face to tell. I definitely cried. They were tears of joy. I went up to my room and put on my best button-down shirt, came back and mixed us all a round of iced tea, because I knew what had happened.

We had just become Air-Conditioner People.

To this day, although my father lives in a town house that

came with the central air conditioning built in, he'll refuse to turn it on. And if you ever sleep there, and you wake up in the middle of the night, confused and sweaty, you might catch him in your room plugging in a portable fan.

And that's all you'll get.

HAVE YOU EVER WORKED
SO MANY DAYS IN A ROW
THAT YOU PULLED INTO
THE PARKING LOT AND
REALIZED YOU DIDN'T EVEN
KNOW YOU WERE DRIVING?
I HAVE...

YOU WORK TOO HARD

They say that Americans are dumb and lazy, and although we don't actually hear people say it, we know damn well they're thinking it.

While there are plenty of nimrods in our country, for the most part we are not lazy. From what I can see, we work harder than any other people on the planet.

Who works harder? Europeans? Please. I've seen them, sitting seaside, drinking wine, and eating giant pastries filled with chocolate and fresh cream in the middle of a workday. They wander down their tiny cobblestone streets that have never been repaired, go inside their open-air apartments, lie down, and sleep the rest of the day.

Maybe they wake up around five, have an espresso under a shade tree with their friends, and smoke cigarettes until they slowly wake up. By the time they're ready the workday is over and it's time for a cocktail, dinner, and a quick ride on their Vespa to make love to their girlfriend before they come home and have dinner with their family.

Not us. We don't have time for romance on scooters with

exotic, caffeinated lovers. We can't sit around and eat omelets and wait for the butter to melt on our baguettes. We're lucky if we get lunch at all. Can you imagine telling your boss that you are going to spend most of the afternoon taking a nap and making love? He'd laugh, pat you on the back, and tell you to gather up your things.

Germany might be an exception, but even they don't work as hard as we do. Sure, they're always on time and are highly efficient. Big deal. How hard is that when you work only eight hours a day and get two months' vacation?

We don't even have hours. We have jobs to do. Jobs that have to get done no matter what, no matter how long it takes or how many late-night emails and phone calls we have to make. In America you get it done or get out.

We wake up in the dark and work through the night. We do early-morning hours, overnight hours, and overtime. We take 5:00 A.M. flights so we can make a meeting by 10:00, put in a full day, and fly back that night on nothing but pretzel sticks. We take the bus, the train, and commuter jets that are held together with duct tape flown by exhausted pilots and the oldest flight attendants working anywhere in the world.

No wonder we're so damn tired. People are sleeping on the subway standing up. People are nodding off in their cars in parking garages. Americans are so tired that they've figured out how to sleep in the middle of meetings with their eyes wide open like horses with business degrees.

We're pounding energy drinks and Red Bulls just to get through the afternoon.

It's no wonder that Starbucks became the biggest company in the country. We need more fuel. And not one little espresso cup like they have in Italy. We need a bucket-size cup that we can squeeze five shots into, a bunch of sugar, and some pumps of caramel on top because we've got stuff to do.

We don't have time for French cafés where everyone sits around and complains about the evils of capitalism. We pick up our coffee at the drive-through on our way to work because we're late on our rent from all the money we spend on lattes.

If it means getting a job, Americans are ready to sacrifice, scrape, and claw their way to it. It's amazing how far we'll go for work. Our freeways, highways, and bus stops are filled with millions of people who for some reason don't live anywhere near where they work. Every day there's an endless migration of people in their cars, eating breakfast, putting on makeup, drinking smoothies, and snorting coffee beans, all while steering with their knees. It's a stop-and-start struggle all the way to the office, and every year the traffic gets worse. Do we move? Hell, no. We just get up earlier.

Americans stay up late and get up in the dark. The alarm goes off at the last possible minute, and immediately we turn into volunteer firemen. Don't even think about pressing the snooze button. Never press the snooze button. It's a lie. A tease. All it does is promise you more sleep while making you later and creating more panic. And that's what the mornings are in this country—pure panic.

Every morning it's as if we're thrown into a natural disaster. We have no choice but to stumble to the bathroom, crawling, banging into the walls, taking deep breaths, confused, blind, and tired. Oh so tired. This is not when the body wanted to wake up. This is when it was forced to wake up like a dog being Tasered awake at the kennel.

There's nothing more important than the shower. A self-shocking system that if skipped will ruin your entire day. Humans should come with a label that reads, "Just Add Water." But this isn't one of those long enjoyable showers when you hug yourself under cascading water while sniffing the soap. This is a speed shower where you do your best to hit the important parts and keep going. This is an ass-and-armpits nuclear reactor shower. They get longer showers in prison.

This is painful. This is misery. You'd love to call in sick, but you can't because you did that last week and they thought you were lying. If you do it now, they'll know for sure.

You want breakfast? Sure, you can have breakfast. But there's no time to sit and read the paper, casually skimming through every section of the newspaper. This is a workday and every second counts. You can't be late. Not in this country. Maybe in Tuscany when you're showing up to your noodle-making job, but not here at Best Buy. Throw on your polo, shine up your name tag, grab a banana, and get out the damn door.

And it's hard work. Important work that keeps everything going, and I'm in awe of you all. Day after day, doing jobs that are so crucial to all our lives. Everything we do throughout our day was touched in some way by another human being doing their job.

Thank God for you all.

Thank God for the guy who drives the Oreos to the store on the corner. Thank God for the cookie maker, the filling person, the packaging lady, and the dude who puts them all in rows.

Someone made my desk. Someone made this computer. Shaped this coffee cup and wrote, "World's Greatest Dad" on it. Someone picked and roasted these coffee beans. Someone designed this chair and figured out how to make the air conditioner work and put the vent in just the right spot so it cools me off but doesn't blow directly on my bald spot.

All hail the people out there making the pens and pencils and my Cambridge pads. You see a mass of people causing traffic? I see heroes going out there every day, doing their part, and making our lives a little better. Like bees in a hive, we all have our job to do. It takes teamwork to make the beehive work.

I'm not saying everyone does their job well. Some do a bad job. We'll never meet them, but we'll feel their effect. Why did that hair dryer break so quickly? Why did the garage door get stuck? Why are all the chips crushed in that bag? Because someone screwed up. Someone didn't take pride in their work, and by not caring about themselves, they don't care about us, and now there is a kink in the system. Now we're just a little more messed up than we should be.

But there's nothing more impressive than when someone does his or her job well.

It's a beautiful thing. I have the most amazing plumber. He loves what he does, he knows what he's doing, and he's a pleasure to watch.

He crawls under the house like a cat. Like a chubby, middle-aged feline. He follows the pipes, inspects as he goes, and finds the problem. My favorite part is when he tells me about it.

"Okay, buddy, I find out the trouble," he says with pride. "Let me explain to you."

He goes into great detail, like a surgeon explaining what he found when he cut open my chest, and I love every minute because he loves what he does.

Americans are doing a great job all over. We're picking almonds and avocados in California. Shooting movies in Atlanta. Selling insurance in Hartford. We fill up office buildings and suites and work from home. We teach children and bake bread and wait on tables and toss drunken people out of bars. These are jobs. Really hard jobs.

Your hard work is the reason our lights stay on, our hospitals are open, and our showers have water pressure. You pave our roads. You police our streets.

When stuff catches on fire because some dingbat doesn't know how to turn on a gas grill, someone does their job and puts it out.

When we are hungry, there are places open at all times of the day and night ready to feed us. When things go wrong, workers are standing by ready to help. Tow trucks, mechanics, and twenty-four-hour help lines.

You may not love your job. Not everyone does. But that doesn't mean you're not doing great work. You are. Right now there is someone cleaning a toilet. Mopping up after some drunk's bad behavior. Carrying garbage, digging holes, pulling out asbestos. Someone is standing in a hot tollbooth on the New Jersey Turnpike. Someone else is pulling weeds in a hot field. Picking strawberries. Demolishing a basement. Riding on the back of a garbage truck. Painting, brushing, cleaning, hosing down, ripping apart, carrying, hauling, raking, and sorting. Every day. All day. All night.

So don't let anyone tell you that you aren't doing enough. That our generation is lazy. That Americans are lazy. Sure, we may not know all the artists in the museums and all the poets from the last century. But that's not because we're slacking off, it's because we're at work, working harder than everybody else. Except maybe all those people in Asia.

HAVE YOU EVER EATEN SO MANY BUFFALO WINGS IN ONE SITTING THAT YOU ALMOST SNEEZED FEATHERS? I HAVE . . . .

SHUT UP AND EAT

I can't stop eating. I won't stop eating. You can't *make* me stop eating.

When I'm eating with other people and reach the end of the meal, it's totally an act. I don't get full. I stop eating only when I can tell that it would be socially unacceptable to keep going. I see people who stop eating when there's still food on their plate and I can only imagine they have something really wrong with them.

I may have a tapeworm. If I find out that I do, I won't have him removed, I'll give him a nickname and call him my friend.

If I'm at a party and there's food out, I lose my mind. If there's a bowl of chips, it's mine. If I see cheese and crackers, you better keep your hands clear or you will get bit. Don't expect me to carry on a conversation when there's a platter of anything around, I simply can't concentrate. Not until my wife drags me into the other room, throws a pitcher of water in my face, and slaps me around.

If we're ever out to dinner together and the waiter asks, "Would you like anything else?" and I say, "No," I'm lying. The real me, the honest me, would always say through a mouth full of something, "Yes, more of everything."

I love food in such a deep, profound way that I'm salivating just writing about it.

There are sandwiches from my past that I carry with me as if they were memories of lovers. "The Italian Special" from Casa Del Sole in Hillsdale, New Jersey. "The Spicy Dom" at Domingo's in Encino, California. "The Michelangelo" from Alidoro on Sullivan Street in New York City.

How did this happen to me? How did I become a fine-food piranha? It's nature and nurture and cheese. The nature is that I come from an Italian family. The nurture is that my Italian family taught me to eat every meal as if it would be my last. And cheese, well, what more can I say?

Italians use food as sport, religion, a career, therapy, and a nonstop celebration.

They are constantly thinking about food, going to get the food, making the food, and feeding everybody the food. Whenever we're eating, all anybody talks about is what we're eating next. Italians truly love life, but that's only because staying alive means they can eat more food.

My childhood was filled with lasagna, meat sauce, and family who kissed me with cannoli on their lips. When we drove to my grandmother's house on Sundays, the smell of garlic and provolone would roll out of her kitchen and open the car door for us. It would take me by the arm and escort me inside, where she would be making a five-course meal out of one can of crushed tomatoes.

There was very little money but a lot of people to feed. I'm one of twenty-three grandchildren and we were all there, at the same time, leaving her no choice but to perform a miracle out of her tiny kitchen each week.

Today people do much less with much more. Modern kitchens

with marble islands, industrial-strength ovens, double freezers, and built-in refrigerators, and no one cooks! Millions of dollars just so they can heat things up. All she had was her small oven and very little counter space, but with the help of the grandchildren learning by her side while washing the pots and pans, it hummed like a fine restaurant.

The dining room was a converted porch where the family ate at a long table, always covered in a crisp white tablecloth. Three generations, united by her cooking, listening, loving, and eating. There seemed to be endless bowls of spaghetti and meatballs, marinated olives, and garlic bread. Chicken Parmesan, homemade ravioli, and gnocchi in heavy cream sauce.

The adults drank wine and snuck it to the children. They would never give it to their own kids but would sneak it to their nieces and nephews, which meant that eventually everyone got some.

I was ten years old, drunk on wine, and covered in sauce. You don't live this way and learn to eat like this without developing a nice, healthy food addiction.

My father and I took it one step further by joining forces in taking on eating challenges. He would take me to White Castle, a dingy fast-food joint that makes Taco Bell seem like dining at the Ritz-Carlton. They're still around and continue to serve the very same square burgers in little cardboard sleeves. You slide them out of the packaging and eat each one in about two bites. At twenty-seven cents apiece we would get sacks of burgers and sit in the car with the cartons spread all around us steaming up the windows. We'd plow through fifty of those suckers without a problem.

My father was always on the lookout for food challenges where he knew we would more than get our money's worth.

He'd heard about an all-you-can-eat sushi place, in Hacken-sack, New Jersey. This was in the 1980s, when sushi wasn't very well known and the offer was their way to get sheltered people from New Jersey to pay attention to this exotic Asian cuisine.

It was a terrible business decision on their part. We plowed through trays of this stuff as fast as they could roll it. My father felt speed was important because he always feared it was just a matter of time before they realized their mistake and changed the rules.

"You're taking too many bites," he'd say. "One bite, swallow. One bite, swallow."

We ate in a panic while the staff stared at us from the kitchen in disbelief.

There are restaurants all around the metropolitan area with our names engraved on the walls in honor of the damage we did. One was an old roadhouse in northern New Jersey, called Joe McDonald's Steakhouse, that had a hard-to-beat steak challenge. It was famous for all the World War II memorabilia that covered every inch of the place. Large men ate large cuts of meat surrounded by thousands of guns, uniforms, and war bond posters.

I loved this place and had been going with my family since I was a little kid, but when I was sixteen they came up with the McDonald's Steak Challenge. If you ate a seventy-two-ounce steak in one sitting, with the sides, you got your name on the wall and a T-shirt with the picture of a cow on it. Despite the hefty carnivores who ate there, not many had won. We wanted to win. We wanted to be on the wall, but even more we wanted the T-shirt. My father would have seen it as a great insult if someone else in town was walking around in that shirt thinking they could eat more than us.

The waitress served the giant dishes with a side dish of disgust.

"You're going to make yourself sick," she said.

"Don't listen to her, Tom, she's trying to mess with your head," my father said.

It was the biggest steak I had ever seen. I quickly understood why there weren't more people with their name engraved on the wall between the hand grenades and bayonets. Eating the steak alone was impossible. Eating the sides as well, insane.

We finished it in five minutes.

"Look, we're even eating the skin," I told the waitress while holding up a potato. She shook her head and handed in her apron.

We are on that wall. I lost the T-shirt.

When I was in college there was the Gaetano's Cheesesteak Challenge. The upperclassmen told us tales of these gigantic sandwiches that were so big they came in beer case boxes. They told us, "No one has ever eaten a whole one. It's impossible."

I quietly smiled to myself.

We drove an hour to the shop and placed our orders. There were no tables, so we all stood around the hood of our car with our sandwiches laid out before us. They were enormous, way too much food for one person. Everyone grew quiet as they struggled to chew. I dabbed the corner of my mouth with a napkin and before anyone was halfway done said, "I'm going for another one, anyone want anything?"

One of my friends passed out. I ate two.

I could be so fat. I'm a little overweight. I'd say happily overweight. Not health problem overweight, but technically, according to my doctor, I could lose a few. I actually got in shape for a physical recently, and while my doctor was proud of my progress, he told me, "Keep it up, only twenty more pounds to go."

There's no way I'm doing it. I don't think it's possible. My metabolism is so slow that in order to lose that weight I would literally have to stop eating altogether. If I starve, I'll maintain the weight I am, yet if I eat one M&M, I'll double in size.

And here's the real reason why I won't take my doctor's advice: I love eating too much. Eating is my life. There's too much happiness and history to put an end to it. I tried to clean up my diet and become a vegetarian. I lasted a while but eventually broke, not for any other reason than that I walked into an Italian deli. All the joyful smells of my entire life wrapped around me, and before I knew it I was walking out the door with boxes filled with cheeses, breads, and prosciutto. I had to steer with one hand because I had a meatball sandwich in the other.

I know I'm not alone in this food passion. It's not as if Italians make up the entire population of the United States. The South is covered in fried chicken, okra, and barbecue. The Southwest is steeped in Mexican heritage. Chinatown is a part of every city. New England raised entire generations on lobster rolls. I was touring in the Upper Midwest in early fall and it was as if someone broke open a bakery case and doughnuts, pies, and maple syrup spilled all the way up to Canada. Wisconsin is literally made out of cheese curds.

It's really our duty to eat and enjoy ourselves. Who cares if you're a little fat? We're all fat. You're either really fat, kind of fat, or trying not to be fat. Either way, fat's coming.

So enjoy yourself. More wine! More bread! More cheese! Do it for you. Do it for your ancestors. Do it for me.

HAVE YOU EVER GOTTEN
A TEXT OF A MONKEY
IN A BIRTHDAY HAT AND
REALIZED IT WAS ACTUALLY
A PICTURE OF YOU AT A
PARTY LAST WEEKEND?
I HAVE....

A VERY FUNNY NOSE

Whenever you look at yourself in the mirror and you are horrified with how ugly you are, just remember that you're not alone. We are all funny-looking. Every single, misshapen, twisted, warped, crooked, spectacularly irregular one of us.

When they say we're all unique snowflakes, that no two of us are alike, that's not because we're all perfectly beautiful, it's because we're flawed in the most hilarious ways.

We've got funny eyes, curled lips, and weird hairlines. Chins that point out, chins that look like a baboon's ass, some of us have no chin at all. Some of us were born without the parts that everyone else has. No eyebrows, no ass, and teeny-weeny noses. How about the no-lip people? They look like the rest of their head is in 3-D with a pencil-sketched mouth.

Our ears are always a mess. Hairy ears, little ears, and ears that stick out on the side. Little ears bother me, they're not fun at all. I have a friend who has little ears with no lobe. It's like her ears are attached directly to her head and someone forgot to trim them.

I love really big ears. Especially on little kids. Big satellite dishes that look like they're trying to catch a signal from a distant planet. They always make me laugh. The best part is you can't hide big ears, all you can do is try and grow your hair long and develop a sense of humor.

We've all got our thing, every single one of us, except of course that one exception. The only one human being who has achieved divine perfection: Gwyneth Paltrow. If you think I'm joking, you are wrong. If you say anything bad about her, I'll punch you right in your cowardly face.

But the rest of us are circus freaks.

What a nice thing to know. Isn't it a relief? Think about how much time I just saved you in the morning. Now, when you look in the mirror, the only thing that should go through your mind is, "Good enough!"

Even the people we see on the covers of magazines, who seem to have a perfect face, are funny-looking. Not at the newsstand all airbrushed and smiley, but at home with the makeup off, they look just like you and me; like monkeys trying their best to evolve.

I'm funny-looking in myriad ways. I have a head that really belongs on a porpoise: a lot of forehead, a little too much chin, and a bald spot that looks like a blowhole. Depending on what angle you catch me at, I have between two and seventeen chins. And I have a patch of hair on my back. It's one patch on the left side, in the shape of New York State and about the size of a frisbee. It's been there since puberty. Actually it started out as a birthmark when I was a child and it eventually turned into hair. Try putting that on a dating profile.

In college my roommate named it, as if it were a third student sleeping in our dorm room. He named it Sammy. I wrote a song about him.

Sammy on my back
Sammy on my back
Whatcha doing there
With all that hair
Sammy!

I also have a big nose. Well, not exactly a big nose, more a fat nose with nostrils that look more like two bat caves than something that belongs on someone's face.

They're so big I made a habit of seeing what I could fit up there. It became a bit of a parlor trick that I would perform for my friends and was always a big hit, until eventually I went too far.

That's when I got a pachinko ball stuck up my nose.

When I was twelve my father bought a pachinko machine at a flea market.

Pachinko is a Japanese, upright pinball machine. It's a very odd game where you pull a lever and a large ball bearing flies into action, ricochets off a thousand tiny nails, and randomly either lands in a spot that awards you more points or fails. There is literally no skill involved, but it's very addicting in a slot machine kind of way.

My father didn't buy a lot of things on a whim. He wasn't the type to bring something home just for the fun of it. He was pretty frugal and only bought stuff that was either absolutely necessary or solely for him, which made the purchase of a Japanese pinball machine very odd. The weirdness of this device might have been the allure, in the same way you would buy a vintage typewriter or an old radio from the 1930s. But more realistically, he must have gotten a really good deal on it or more likely he found it at the dump.

He brought it home and put it in the basement, and we

played with it for hours. Days. *Years.* But as the game itself was kind of boring, we eventually started playing with the pachinko balls themselves. We'd gather them up from the back and throw them at each other, roll them around, and eventually I got the hilarious idea to stick one up my nose.

When I would perform one of these nose tricks, I wouldn't just stick it up there straightaway. I wasn't an amateur. I learned how to build suspense from Evel Knievel, the great motorcycle daredevil. He never blasted off a jump the first time out. He was a master showman who knew how to expertly tease the audience. He'd adjust his helmet, climb on his bike, and work the crowd into a frenzy with every rev of his engine. Everyone would anticipate his jump as he raced down the ramp, and just when he should've been accelerating he'd come to a sudden stop at the edge. The crowd would go crazy. He'd shake his head, turn the bike around, and head back to the start while the crowd lost its collective mind. Evel didn't give you what you wanted when you wanted it. This was his show, on his terms.

I was the Evel Knievel of nose tricks. I held the pachinko ball in my hand. "Is it possible? Can it be done?" The crowd, which consisted of my two friends Keith and Dave, went crazy.

The funny thing about kids, when they're watching their friend about to do something stupid, is the complete lack of concern for their well-being. Never in the history of childhood has there been a cautionary pal who tells you to slow down and reconsider what you are doing. Never.

The response to any life-threatening endeavor, be it jumping out of a tree house, flying your bike off a jump, or sticking a metal pachinko ball in your nasal cavity, is always the same: "Do it!"

That's what they chanted as they clapped, danced, and threw themselves on the ground.

"Do it! Do it!"

I had worked them into a complete and proper frenzy.

I held the ball up one last time. They gasped. I posed. They fell silent. Slowly I moved the ball toward the edge of my nostril—and inhaled. The gigantic ball fired straight up my nose, way too fast, way too easily, and way too deep. This antique metal ball bearing, which had entertained Asian pinball fans for more than fifty years, was now in the upper reaches of my nasal cavity entertaining my friends like never before.

The crowd went nuts.

I had a fleeting moment of victory, followed by a brief pause. And then panic. The room went silent. My friends leaned in. My eyes darted around. We hung there in space, trying to piece together what exactly was happening, and we all realized at the exact same moment—that it was stuck!

It wasn't coming out. I was in real trouble. Keith and Dave were laughing harder than they had in their entire lives. They were rolling around on the floor and hitting each other with delight.

I was caught in a slight two-step where I knew I should be running for help but didn't know where to go, so instead I just bounced from side to side. I dug my finger up, I felt the ball, but there was no room around the sides of it. It was wedged in tight and my poking around had only pushed it up even higher.

I was scared, but my friends were so extremely happy that I started laughing, too. I couldn't help it. This was ridiculous. I had a pachinko ball stuck in my nose. The laughter calmed me down and enabled me to see more clearly.

With my friends at my feet, I used my finger to close off the other nostril and with all my might tried to blow the pachinko ball out of my head.

"What is he doing now?" Keith cried.

"Oh no," said Dave.

At first it seemed hopeless. All I was doing was building up so much pressure that I was turning red. Keith was laughing so hard that he couldn't speak. All he could do was point at me with tears of joy running down his face.

I took a deep breath, tilted my head back, and pushed with all my might. I turned from red to purple and then something squeaked like a pinched balloon and the pachinko ball fired from my face like a bullet.

It was more powerful than any BB gun I had ever fired. The ball shot out of my nose, across the room, and off the wall, ricocheting around, turning the basement into a life-size pachinko machine.

I was saved. Dave and Keith laughed for another three days. I was a hero.

And none of this would have been possible if I hadn't embraced that big, fat nose of mine and celebrated myself. I became a legend on that day. All thanks to my very funny nose.

So embrace your flaws. All of you. The girl with the ski-slope nose. The man with the pineapple head and beady eyes. And you with the fish lips. Own it. Enjoy it.

You're beautiful.

NANCY AND EMILY

The first girl I ever fell in love with smelled like sweat and bug spray. We were two kids, running and playing throughout our neighborhood for the entire summer. Her name was Nancy. She was sweet and fun and we were in first or second grade. We did everything together. We'd play ball, run through the woods, and sit by the side of the brook that ran through the back of our school, skimming rocks and catching crawfish. We did everything that growing kids do when they're exploring the world and themselves.

But unlike other friends, we were both aware that this was a special friend. She was a girl. I was a boy. Which meant that we could also do something else. We weren't exactly sure what that something was, but it was something that made us giggle and wrestle around on the lawn under the low-hanging willow tree because no one could see us there and whatever it was we were doing or trying to do, we knew enough to keep it a secret.

That secret got out one day when her mother saw us playing around, innocently enough, but not completely without cause for concern, and that was all it took. An adult had dragged our behavior out into the open by ordering us around with that stern adult tone and we knew the fun was over and we should probably be ashamed. Eden was lost.

From that point on I was fascinated with girls. I knew there was so much to learn and I wanted to know everything I could. I was interested in what they were talking about, what they were thinking, and why they cried. And I loved making them laugh.

I knew that if I showed them that I cared, that I truly cared, they would open up like a book with hidden chapters and let me read it all. Boys didn't do that. Boys didn't share. Boys hit and were taught to stay silent. I knew what boys were made of; I was a boy and I was unimpressed.

I didn't chase after another girl until I was in fifth grade and fell in love with Emily. She was poised and very pretty, with long black hair. She sat next to me in class and I was infatuated. Her family had moved from the Philippines. She was restrained and didn't want to get in trouble, so I worked extra hard at making her laugh in the middle of class. The way she would cover up her smile with her hand, and try not to look at me because she knew she'd lose control, excited me in a thousand ways.

I had watched enough TV to know that I needed to give her a fancy gift, because that's what men did. From what I could gather, after a man falls in love with a gal, he takes her out for food and gives her jewelry. But those men also had jobs and money and they knew where the jewelry stores were. I had none of that. But what I did have was a mother. A mom who had a very unorganized drawer that was filled with a lot of costume jewelry. That was the first jewelry shopping I ever did: sneaking into my mother's room and looking for just the right thing for Emily.

I knew Emily liked the finer things. She wore flat little shoes like the other girls in class, but hers had little sparkly pearls on them. I needed to pick something out that was elegant, refined, and yet youthful. And more important, something that my mother wouldn't notice was missing.

I picked out a beaded blue necklace that had a turquoise bird on it. It was toward the bottom of the drawer, tangled up with some other forgotten necklaces. I was pretty sure Emily would like it. I thought she probably liked blue, and everybody likes birds.

I found a box, stuck the necklace in it, and snuck it into my book bag. I carried it all the way to school as if I were carrying the Hope Diamond. If I'd had handcuffs, I would have used them to attach myself to the bag and hired my friends as bodyguards. Only I couldn't tell my friends. I couldn't tell anyone what I was about to do. I had never given a girl anything before and I was already growing nervous and humiliated at the same time. This was way beyond my skill level.

I sat with it for the entire day, waiting for a moment when we could be alone. It wasn't until class was out that I caught up to her in the hallway. I asked if we could talk, which already made things too formal and more than a little weird. This was beginning to feel like a mistake, but it was too late to turn back.

I quickly handed her the box.

"What's this?"

"It's a present."

"Why?"

"I don't know."

She grimaced as she opened it. What looked like a good idea at home now in her hand looked like a weird old-lady necklace. It was something a crazy aunt would show off as a "real steal" that she picked up at a flea market dollar table.

"What is this?"

"That's a bird."

"It doesn't look like a bird. It looks like a rock."

She was right. Not only did it not look like a bird, but when she held the necklace up it was obvious that it was way too long. This wasn't going well. She didn't know how to react. I thought I was giving her a gift, and now it felt like I was tormenting her. Her direct honesty, which I always admired, was about to come out and slap me around.

"It's kind of gross," she said as she picked some fuzz off it.

I couldn't respond. And then she asked me the most honest question that anyone had ever asked when I was giving them a gift.

"Can you take it back?"

As I returned it that night, looking at the other necklaces in the box I could have given her, I realized it had nothing to do with the jewelry I had chosen. I had picked the wrong girl. A girl who didn't like me as much as I liked her. I had naïvely put myself out there, dangling off the edge of a cliff, fully confident that it would work out, and I had plunged to my death. I hadn't even considered that rejection was a possibility.

Of course, this wasn't the last time this would happen. My life is filled with mistakes great and not so small. But I knew even then that no matter how much it hurt, I had to keep trying.

Emily stopped laughing at my jokes. During class she turned the other way. We were through. But then I looked across the room and saw Suzanne. She was cute, with light freckles and brown hair that came down to her eyes. She looked up, caught me staring, and as she smiled back, I thought, "I bet *she'd* think it looked like a bird."

HAVE YOU EVER WORN YOUR BATHING SUIT TO A POOL PARTY AND WHEN YOU GOT THERE REALIZED IT WASN'T A POOL PARTY? I HAVE....

FUN THINGS THAT AREN'T

Here's a tip for you: Don't do what other people tell you is a good time. It never is.

A perfect example—breakfast in bed. It's a horrible idea. And yet every poor mother on Mother's Day has to get a tray filled with hard toast and runny eggs, and we pin her down in her bed. "Enjoy your breakfast like a hospital patient. Good luck not spilling the juice on your nightgown. We'll be at IHOP, see you in an hour."

I understand wanting to have fun, trying to find a good time, but this should be a personal decision. I really like sitting on my couch. That's it. No book, no TV, no phone, no friends. Just sitting on my couch. This is fun for me. And I discovered it all by myself.

Do you know what's not fun for me? Candy apples.

Candy apples are another horrible lie about a good time. They're awful. First off, they've got it all backward. Why would you put fruit on the inside of candy? So you do all this work, get through the candy outside, and your reward is a mealy apple? What kind of incentive is that? How about if you get through the world's most boring fruit, the apple, you're rewarded with a candy center? At least you have something to work for.

The world is filled with terrible "fun-filled" ideas. The ultimate is cruise ships. Please, stop with the cruise ships. It's a dumb idea of a good vacation. Anything you can do on that dumb boat you can do here on land. Lame magic shows, waterslides, buffets, it's all here. You don't need to go to the middle of the ocean, where you do not belong, floating around in a giant white toilet.

That's all these stupid boats are. They're giant white toilets ruining the seas. What does everybody talk about on these dumb ships? The food.

"Oh, the food. They give you seven meals a day. They take your three meals and they add four more to it."

Sure, and then what does everybody do? They wander off to their room and take a dump in the sea.

Stop it.

I was in Italy in this tiny little town. You couldn't fit one more person in this village. Every table was booked and every room was occupied. In the middle of dinner, a giant cruise ship pulled into port. It was the scariest thing I ever saw. The locals knew what was coming. Mothers were barricading themselves into their homes with their children, lovers were hiding in coffee shops, even the police disappeared.

The gangplank came down and this army of tourists came waddling out in their Tommy Bahamas and their flip-flops as if it were an invasion. They beat the locals with selfie sticks and gobbled up all the souvenirs. They trampled through the streets, ate everything they could find, went back on the boat, and took another dump in the sea.

Stop it.

And what about all the diseases? Every year there's a shocking report of yet another outbreak of a poop virus, food virus, and the latest version of *E. coli* on another Fun-Filled Cruise Line.

This is caused by vacation behavior. Vacation behavior is drunk behavior. It's "let it all hang loose" behavior. It's "walk around all day in your bathing suit drinking mai tais" behavior.

When we're on vacation we become different people. That's why people go. To get away from it all, including themselves. They leave behind the worker bee, who is filled with responsibility, obligations, and family members, and go nuts.

I was in Hawaii last year and I saw a businessman checking in at the front desk, dressed in his tie and hard black dress shoes. He whipped out his credit card, negotiated for a better room, and tipped the bellboys. He was a man and he was all business.

Six hours later, I saw him sitting on the top of a waterslide in his boxer shorts, a shell necklace, and a piña colada the size of his leg. He was changed. He was not a businessman. He was an animal. He wasn't thinking about work, he was thinking about all-you-can-eat poolside nachos. He was purple with sunburn and he didn't care. He was too drunk to care. He had nowhere to go, no boss to talk to, nothing but good times and really bad behavior.

Now, you want to take three thousand other human beings in the same state of mind and squish them all onto a boat together where they can't escape? Yech.

Look, in a resort, for a little while, it can be a blast. I'm not saying you can't have a fun time. And I'm not saying you can't be around other people. I'm not even saying that you shouldn't act like an idiot.

To paraphrase Walt Whitman, "We are large. We contain multitudes." We have all been the best person in the room and the worst person in the room. I have been a rube and I have been a poet. I have been a monster and I have been an angel. One thing I won't be is trapped on a giant ship while drunk people throw up all around me. That's not fun.

Anytime someone says to me, "Come on, it'll be fun," I run the other way.

Some things are fun once. When you're young and you try something for the first time, it can actually be a lot of fun. Miniature golf, bowling, badminton, and lawn darts. Karaoke, roller-skating, and Ferris wheels. Giant lollipops, 3-D glasses, and board games. All these are fun when you're a child because you don't know any better. It's a surprise.

But as an adult you've done it all before and you know exactly what's going to happen if you accept an invitation to play miniature golf. You're going to get there; there will be some excitement as you pick out your putter, a golf ball, and a tiny pencil. You'll play the first hole and have some laughs. And then you'll stand there, with a miniature club in your hand, waiting for the people ahead of you to finish up, and you suddenly realize you have *seventeen more holes to go*!

You've been trapped because you didn't think for yourself.

All I'm saying is have fun, but in your own way, that's individual to you. Let the crowd run off and stand in line for bowling shoes. I'll be having twice as much fun, by myself, sitting on my couch.

HAVE YOU EVER TRIED TO
GET BACK AT YOUR DENTIST
BY SHOWING UP FOR
YOUR CLEANING WITH A
MOUTHFUL OF CHEETOS?
I HAVE....

IT TAKES TWO

From what I can tell, the real reason to find someone and fall in love and move in together and share calendars and a bed is so that when you're old you'll have someone who can help get you to your next doctor's appointment.

Whenever I have some sort of medical appointment of my own, I always see older couples helping each other along. And it looks like it really takes two to get there. Leaving the house when you're old takes as much courage as jumping out of a plane when you're younger. It's daunting, high risk, and there's a good chance you won't make it back.

I see them side by side, holding each other up like cartoon drunks, forging ahead, conquering all the treacherous obstacles in their way: parking lots, curbs, heavy doors, building directories, vaguely marked elevator keys, stairs, a loose paper cup blown across their path. It's a minefield out there.

Even driving is a two-person job at that point. Like soldiers driving a tank together, each has a role to play. One sits up high on a pile of books in big dark glasses, taking care of the lookout and the steering. The other, through a series of verbal commands, handles the stuff down below, working the radio and the directional and pushing on the pedals with her hands.

This is something I've tried to keep in mind when I lose my patience on the road. There are a lot of cars making insane moves out there, and for years I figured they were being driven by people much like myself, only dumber, drunker, and more inconsiderate. While this could be true, a larger number are just terrible drivers because they are either very young or very old. The inexperienced drivers are encountering fresh challenges every time they head down the road. Every pothole, parked car, and squirrel represents a new, terrifying event. And the old people have seen it all, dealt with it all, and can't remember a thing about it.

It must be terrifying driving under the influence of extreme age. Contrary to what my kids think, I'm not old by any means, and already my skills are waning. I have the eyesight of a nearsighted mole rat. I'm not as bad as that old cartoon character Mr. Magoo, but he's suddenly not as funny to me. For my entire life, my eyes were amazing. I would read signs from miles away, especially in front of old people just to rub it in.

I think back on all those times my mother yelled at me to stop reading in the dark and I'd just laugh, knowing full well that I had the eyes of a bat. But maybe she was right. Maybe that's why my eyes aren't so great today—a mix of reading in the dark and bad karma.

When my eyes started naturally aging and I slowly realized that I needed reading glasses, I started noticing that one eye was worse than the other. After a year or so of self-diagnosing at the CVS while picking up ChapStick and sunblock, I decided that maybe I should go to a real eye doctor.

It was time for a real doctor's appointment all by myself.

My good friend referred me to her doctor on New York's

Upper East Side. This sat very well with me. The Upper East Side is filled with a lot of old, rich people who go only to the best doctors. I don't often equate quality with money, but in the instance of health care I do. You show me a doctor who can afford the rent on Fifth Avenue and I rest easy.

When I arrived I was met with big heavy doors with iron handles, marble floors, and a doorman. After living in New York for a long time in buildings that hardly had working doors, I found having a doorman very impressive.

I filled out my new-patient forms and listened to the hum of the fish filter while eavesdropping on the other patients. An oboe player from the Metropolitan Opera was complaining that her appointment time would make her late for *Carmen* rehearsal. Only in New York.

When they called my name I entered what looked like a library or a study that just happened to have some medical equipment in it. It was the kind of place where gentlemen of old would retire after dinner to talk about business and safari so as not to offend their wives' dainty ears.

The friendly nurse set me up in front of the giant eye-testing devices and I responded as best I could to which way the "E" was facing and where the hot-air balloon was on the horizon. Although I wasn't perfect, it felt like I was kind of nailing it.

I was led back to the doctor's private office to wait for his arrival. When he came in he was wearing a trench coat, which you really see only in New York, D.C., and London. This is the coat of a grown-up.

He seemed really smart. Not cutting-edge smart, but traditional, "this is the way it's always been done so we're going to keep doing it this way because it's the right way" kind of smart. He checked my hot-air balloon results and all seemed pretty average. And then he grew quiet. He asked me to look into his own equipment.

"Uh-huh . . . hmm . . ."

I started to worry.

"I'm going to dilate your eyes. Have you ever had that done before?"

"No, I have not."

"Okay. It's not a big deal. This will give me a chance to see other parts of the eye."

He hit me with some eyedrops, and after a couple of minutes everything grew blurry. It's not a great feeling.

Back on the machine.

"Wow. Look at that. Did you have an eye injury when you were younger?" he asked.

"I don't think so," I said.

"You definitely had something. . . . Hey, Carol," he said, "come look at this. You don't see this every day."

For a doctor who gave the impression that he's seen everything in his career, this was not good.

She stepped in. "Wow, will you look at that."

"What is it?" I asked, now sweating on the equipment.

"You have a scar on the right cornea. It's like a smudge right in the middle of your eye. I'm really surprised you're able to see as well as you can."

"Is that why it's fuzzy when I look out of that eye?" A stupid question.

"That's right. You must have scratched it pretty badly when you were a kid and now that you're getting older it's coming into play."

"I do remember this one pillow fight that I had when I got really stung in the eye," I blurted out like a moron.

"That might explain it," he said. As if that behavior explained not only my eye smudge but why I didn't get accepted into an Ivy League school and become a doctor. At the same age when he was playing chess and dreaming of medical school, my friend and I were beating each other in the head with pillows.

He put me at ease about my condition, which he explained wouldn't get worse and while not perfect shouldn't pose any future problems. While he spoke, my eyes reached maximum dilation, or in basic terms, I couldn't see squat.

We shook hands and he said goodbye to me a little too loudly, as if my ears were the problem. Carol led me to the desk. I was bumping into things and making jokes, but this was no laughing matter. I really couldn't see. I just picked a random credit card out of my wallet and handed it to the woman at the desk, which may have explained the doorman and the fancy fish tank.

Carol said I could wait in the office while my vision returned, but in that stubborn male way I assured her that I was more than capable of seeing my way out. I had to stop myself from telling her how good my eyes were in high school as I felt for the door.

I guided myself out of the building by memory. As he opened the door, the doorman gave me a New Yorker "See ya later, buddy, unless you see me first."

I laughed, probably in the wrong direction, as the cool breeze told me where the outside of the building was. I headed out onto the street and there I stood. Alone. With no idea of where I was going or how I would get there. I needed my eyes. I needed help.

I needed my wife.

This is how life will be in the future. When my everyday vision, my best vision, will be like this dilated mess. And while my wife's eyes may be better than mine, she'll have her own problems, like a bum hip or weak hearing. But it will be all right. We'll have each other to lean on as we spend the rest of the day making our way back home.

Maybe we'll stop off at the market and pick up an apple or a tuna sandwich that we can split for dinner before watching a show together and turning in early so we can get up at sunrise and head to our next appointment.

Because that's how it goes.

HAVE YOU EVER GOTTEN SO DRUNK ON TEQUILA THAT YOU AND YOUR FRIENDS ATTACKED A TACO BELL AND TRIED TO FREE THE BURRITOS? I HAVE . . .

IT'S BAD FOR YOU AND THAT'S OKAY

I woke up this morning feeling like someone hit me in the head with a hammer and covered my eyes in fiberglass insulation. As I stumbled into the bathroom, confused, unsteady, and trying to remember what I had done to myself the night before and why my tongue tasted like a liver-and-tobacco sandwich, it all came back to me. Simply put, I drank too much.

It's at this moment when we all say to ourselves, "Never again." And then you drag around all day, trying to hydrate and popping Advil, all the while feeling like crap but happy with your decision to take at least a night off. And then five o'clock comes around and without even thinking about it, you find yourself ordering a drink at the bar or mixing a martini in the kitchen.

We love to do things that are bad for us.

The reason for this lapse of judgment is that truthfully I didn't really make the decision not to drink. That was a different guy. That was Morning Tom.

You'd like Morning Tom. Morning Tom is a great guy who gets up early, returns emails, and gets things done. Morning

Tom puts on workout clothes and exercises before the day begins. He takes a blender and fills it with fruit and protein powder and makes fruit smoothies for breakfast.

But then five o'clock rolls around and a different guy shows up. This is Nighttime Tom. And he's a very different guy. He does not work out. He does not care about getting things done. He's concerned only with having a good time, and the fastest way to get that going is to start getting out the ice at 4:58 and the martini shaker at 4:59 so we are guaranteed to be drinking at 5:00. He's an alcoholic, is what he is.

You'd like Nighttime Tom, too. You might even like him more than Morning Tom. He's a lot more fun. He's nothing but fun. He doesn't make smoothies. He takes that same blender and uses it to mix up a batch of margaritas.

But as with all people who are a one-person party, there's a good chance he'll end up in jail. Morning Tom won't call you from prison in the middle of the night, begging you to bring bail money. When the phone rings you can bet it's Nighttime Tom.

It's fascinating that we all have these two personalities inside us. This is the human condition at its most conflicted. One side is responsible and hardworking, plowing through the day, and the other is the bad student who knows just how to get you into trouble.

We're all deviants. We love to wander from the safe and healthy path, in little and big ways. We all have a wild side to us. We are beasts with desires and sometimes lose control, which is why they came up with police, paddy wagons, and the Bible.

But we have to do things that are bad for us. Some of my most memorable moments have been out on the edge. I can't remember a single vegan meal that I got at Whole Foods, but

I sure as hell remember the night my nephew Sam and I spent way too much money at Il Mulino steakhouse eating medium-rare rib eyes after ice-cold martinis and a bottle of Châteauneuf-du-Pape.

Did I remember any of the nights that I went home early and got a good night's sleep? Not really. But I'll never forget when my friends and I were so drunk that we woke up on a boat in the middle of a lake. We didn't know what lake it was, and none of us owned a boat.

I love cheese. I could do a whole book on my love of cheese. And I know without a doubt that cheese is bad for me. Not only because it makes me fat but because I have an allergy to dairy products that makes my sinuses explode.

For years I thought I was allergic to cats, mold, trees, weeds, and old people. But after years and years of blowing my nose and sneezing like a crazy person, the culprit turned out to be dairy products.

I discovered this by mistake, after TV's Marilu Henner told me to cut it out of my diet along with meat, alcohol, and sugar. That's a weird statement. She didn't tell me directly, but we were on *The View* at the same time. That's an even weirder statement. Actually she was a guest on the show and I had come in to do audience warm-up. It went horribly wrong.

Allow me to explain.

I was a young comedian and at the time never woke up before noon, but I got an offer to fill in for the warm-up comic on *The View* at 7:00 A.M. I had never done anything like this, but I was poor, my girlfriend wanted to go, and I took the job. I shouldn't have.

I was building a career in smoke- and curse-filled nightclubs and now I was thrust into a studio filled with morning-television enthusiasm. I didn't belong there. I also had no idea what I was doing or how I should do it.

They handed me a microphone and told me to "be funny" and "keep the audience energized" in between segments and during the commercial breaks. My way of being funny at the time was telling distasteful, somewhat dirty material about living in New York. No one at *The View* was asking for this.

They cut to commercial and I came sauntering out, with sleepy eyes, a wrinkled shirt, and told an off-color joke. No one responded. I mocked someone's shirt in the front row. Now I was just mean. The entire audience of nice suburban moms looked at me as if I had broken into their house and was peeing on the carpet.

I started to sweat.

The show came back from commercial again and I sat on the side, trying to think of what to do. My girlfriend smiled weakly and patted me on the back. That's not something people do when things are going well. I was desperately trying to come up with some joke that would work as they threw to another break.

"I know," I thought to myself as I walked back out. "I'll do the joke about long nipples."

I gave it my best. A woman gasped. The crowd shifted in their seats. A security guard put his hand on his gun, not sure if he should do something. I was going down in flames.

That's when I saw Barbara Walters, who was the main host at the time and a national treasure, walking slowly toward me shaking her head. At eighty years old, this woman who had seen her share of national tragedies now had her sights set on me. I wasn't sure what was happening. I thought that maybe she was going to support me and tell the crowd how funny I was. But as she got closer I heard her muttering under her breath, "No, no, no," and she took the microphone out of my hand.

"That's enough," she said. The crowd applauded.

I sat back down. My girlfriend looked the other way. Any confusion and hurt that I felt was only made worse when Marilu Henner came out to promote her new diet book, to wild screams and applause. Order had been restored. Barbara had saved the show. The crowd really went berserk when they found out that everybody was getting a free copy of the book. Even the inappropriate comedian who seemed to be there only to sweat and annoy people got one, too.

I swallowed my pride and read the book, or rather listened to my girlfriend talk about the book, and we followed her advice. For a month, we went off alcohol, sugar, dairy, and meat.

It became clear that dairy was a huge part of my diet, and it was killing me not to eat it. But as I tried to abstain, I discovered an amazing thing. I stopped sneezing.

It was over. After decades of blowing my nose, taking pills, and going to doctors, I was actually cured. I could pet my cat in a moldy cellar at the height of allergy season and I was fine. As long as I didn't eat cheese. Cheese is really bad for me.

Thank you, Barbara Walters.

But there was no staying away. Not a chance. I love cheese. Chips, omelets, sandwiches, what good are any of these things without cheese?

Wine and cheese. Cheese and crackers. Burger and cheese. There's no way I was stopping. I'd rather blow my nose every day.

This is a perfect example of something I know is bad for me. It makes me sneeze, it makes me fat, and it probably clogs my arteries and slows my heart. But when I'm holding a slice of Mimolette or spreading blue cheese on a cracker or all over my face, I couldn't care less.

You have to enjoy your life! Too much of a good time and you end up in pain. Too little of a good time and you end up miserable. I don't know anyone who follows all the rules who's fun to hang out with. They might be okay for a while, but soon you'll get bored, and when you do it's time to call that friend who keeps a beer funnel in his car and some cheese in his pocket.

Sorry, Morning Tom.

HAVE YOU EVER GOTTEN BUTT DIALED BY YOUR PARENTS AND FOUND OUT THAT EVEN THOUGH YOU WERE AN ADULT THEY WERE THINKING ABOUT PUTTING YOU UP FOR ADOPTION?
I HAVE . . .

HERE COMES SOME BAD NEWS

While you're trying to maintain a positive attitude and navigate through this stress-filled life, you need to avoid anything that can bring you down. Like phone calls from my mother.

When my mother calls I brace myself for the news that someone has died. And while that might not be why she called this time, that won't stop her from launching through a list of really horrible news. She's scarier than Wolf Blitzer and Fox News combined.

"Did you hear? Uncle Dave fell again. This time he landed on the other wrist, so now he's walking around with casts on both hands. . . . Don't you remember? He fell off the toilet trying to get the bugs out of the light. . . . It's true. I don't even want to know how he's wiping his butt, but you can bet it's Aunt Carol's job now. . . .

"Did you hear about Chris? Her dog has post-traumatic stress disorder. Seems that he was playing in the yard and he sat on a hornet's nest. She saw him through the window running around like crazy and thought he was playing, but he was getting the bejesus stung out of him. Well, she took him to the vet and everything was fine, but now he won't go in the yard. You know Chris and how she is with that dog. She treats the thing better than I treat your father. Well, now she's taking the dog to a therapist. Can you believe that? Therapy for a dog? How the hell does that work? Does the dog lie on a couch and tell secrets about his mother? It's all too much."

At this point I'm starting to look through my liquor cabinet.

"Remember when I told you that Carrie was acting funny at Easter? . . . You don't? Oh yes, you do, don't you remember everyone thought she was cheating on Kevin because she got a new haircut and joined a gym? . . . Well, yes, it does, why else would someone do something like that after they've been married for twelve years? You don't all of a sudden decide to look good for no reason. . . . Oh, really, Mr. Wiseguy, well, guess what? Turns out she's been having an affair with her personal trainer for a year and a half. That's right. I'm always telling your father, those personal trainers are nothing but gigolos. What middle-aged woman needs a personal trainer? What sporting event is she preparing for? I'll tell you what. The 'roll in the sack when your husband is out of town' event. You don't get all sweaty in your yoga pants with a man who isn't your husband unless you're looking for trouble. So anyway, now they're getting the divorce I always thought they'd get. . . .

"Speaking of divorce, did I tell you about your father? He's still with me and refuses to leave. Can you believe the nerve of that man? I've tried everything to get him to go. I stopped doing his laundry, I've stopped feeding him, and he's still sitting over there on the couch like he's the king of Siam. He won't take his medications anymore, not that they ever made a difference. Who cares how high his cholesterol is anyway?

"What he really needs is a pill to make him more handsome. Something that will tighten up some of those chins of his."

Now I'm reaching for a bigger glass.

"Are you coming for Thanksgiving? . . . I don't care that it's summer, we have to plan these things or they don't happen. I'm thinking of having Thanksgiving this year, but I have to be honest, I don't think I can do any of the cooking. . . . Well, who else is going to have it? We can't go to your sister's house, they're under construction again. And you know Mark; he's the champ of starting a project and never finishing it. The poor girl hasn't had a proper roof over her bedroom in two years. He ripped the thing off so he could put in a sunlight. Well, they have real sunlight now, boy. No, we can't have Thanksgiving there or the crows will be coming through the hole in the roof and flying off with the turkey. . . . What do you mean? Why wouldn't a crow eat a turkey? Because it's a bird? That's ridiculous. Everybody loves turkey.

"No, we'll have it at my house and that's that. Everyone can bring something, but not you, of course, Mr. Bigshot who will probably be staying in a hotel because he doesn't love his mother enough to sleep in a twin bed in the guest room. . . . It is not an attic, it's the top floor."

Now I've laid the phone on the counter, started to make a margarita in a blender, and can still hear her from across the room.

"Did you hear what happened to Uncle Bill? He stayed in a roadside motel so he could save an extra five dollars and he was attacked by bedbugs. They ate the skin off both of his legs from the knee down and now he has to walk around with pantyhose on like a drag queen. Aunt Laurie wouldn't let him back in the house because she didn't want to be infested, so he's sleeping in the garage on an old army cot with baseball gloves on his hands like a baby with fingernails so he won't scratch himself all up. Can you picture that? That's got to be some sight. Anyway, you'll see them at Thanksgiving. . . .

"So, everyone will bring something. We'll have a nice time. And if your father is still living here, maybe he can pick up a turkey at the Stop and Shop. . . . Are you there? . . .

"Hello? I can hear you breathing. Why don't you call me more often?"

HAVE YOU EVER CHECKED YOUR BALANCE AT AN ATM AND IT WAS SO LOW THAT YOU HAD TO PRETEND THAT YOU WEREN'T THERE TO TAKE MONEY OUT? I HAVE . . .

YOU'RE RICH!

Money. We're all obsessed with money, stressed about money, and trying to get more money. Money makes the world go round, keeps you above water, and helps you get a new shirt from time to time. But the amount you *really* need is all about perspective and I bet you don't need as much as you think you do.

Look, we all want money. You want enough to take care of your family, get yourself out of trouble, and save for the inevitable rainy days. You should be able to meet your obligations and have enough left over to eat in a nice restaurant, give to charity, or buy a miniature pony to cut the lawn. You should also have enough to buy something stupid from time to time, without your spouse worrying and calling you an idiot. If you're a forty-year-old man and you want to buy an Xbox, you should buy an Xbox. You don't need your wife calling you a moron. You'll find that out in two weeks' time, when you realize you don't have any time for an Xbox because you're a forty-year-old man.

As the old saying goes, "Money can't buy you happiness," but it actually does for a while. It's true that the joy money affords you levels off at some point, but there's a lot of happiness to be had in the space between worrying if you can afford to get your teeth fixed and deciding whether you should buy a limo with a hot tub in it.

There are times in your life when money is truly not important at all. When you're young and poor you don't need much money because you're already rich. You have freedom and you'll never have it again. There were times when I was young that I lived on five dollars a day. That's what I made at the comedy club each night and it was enough. Who needs to worry about getting only five dollars when my favorite bagel with cream cheese cost three dollars?

I loved being young and poor. No possessions, no worries, driving around in an awful car. Remember your glorious first car? I had a Toyota Corolla and it was all kinds of bad. For starters it was baby-shit orange; that's what it said in the brochure. It didn't start half the time but it was light, so I could get a friend to push it, pop the clutch, jump-start it, and away we'd go.

I bought it for twelve hundred dollars that I made myself working as a busboy in a restaurant called the Orchards. My uniform was designed to make me look like a leaf, with green pants, apron, and bow tie. I would wake up in the dark, walk to work, and pour water for businessmen every day, all summer long. It was humiliating, but at the end I had my own car and I was free.

Free to drive to the beach. Free to pick up my girlfriend from her work at the ice-cream shop. Free to enjoy my life with less money in the bank than I spend on lunch today.

If you have a cheap car, enjoy it. You can do anything you want. If you like *Star Wars* and find a plastic Darth Vader head, glue it right to the hood. You can't do that with a leased Mercedes. They won't let you. You can with a used Datsun. You can throw on a

Chewbacca mask, jump in the Vadermobile, and drive the wrong way down the freeway. Everyone will get out of your way because they know you're poor and have nothing to lose.

Those days are long gone for me. I don't have that freedom anymore. I made a horrible business decision. I got married and had two children. I love them, but they just keep growing and getting bigger and asking for more and more money. At this point it's like I'm living with two unemployed coke addicts.

They come into my office every morning: "Hey, can we have some more money?"

"What happened to the change from yesterday?"

"I don't know . . . the economy, am I right?"

No, they're not right, and now I have no freedom at all, because their lives depend on me. Every single day. And I can't tell anyone about it. I just have to swallow the stress and slowly lose my hair. I can't wake my daughter up at two o'clock in the morning, sit on the end of her bed, and say, "Hey, honey. It's me. Didn't mean to wake you, but do you ever feel like you're not going to make it? Like you just can't do it anymore? Ah, forget it, get some sleep, I'll see you at breakfast. If I'm still here."

And I spoil them. I spoil the hell out of them. First off, they're two girls so I don't really have any control over it, they own me. Second, my father didn't spoil us. He had money, but he didn't want to spend it on children. His philosophy was, "I made it, I'm going to use it." He didn't do anything that kids wanted to do. Can you imagine living in a time when the children weren't in charge? It sounds like a magical time to be alive. He took us to an amusement park once, saw the line, and said, "Just look at it through the fence, you get the idea."

My daughters make me take them out for ice cream three times a week and I do it, like an idiot. I'm not making great people, they're pretty entitled. They walk into that ice-cream shop with their thirteen-year-old friends and demand samples with those little sample spoons as if they are ice-cream queens.

"Let me try that one. . . . No. I think you can do better. Let me try that one."

My father took us out for ice cream once. "Everyone gets one scoop of vanilla, no cones, put out your hands."

We were near tears, like grateful characters out of Oliver Twist. "Thank you, Father. This is the most special of days."

You would think that if you made enough money, you could buy that freedom back that you had when you were young, but you're wrong. The more money you make, the more you spend on stupid stuff and the more you grow your life into something bigger, and that bigger life needs even more money. Ultimately you end up more stressed than when you started out.

The trick is to live a small, simple life, but for some reason we aren't built that way. We always want more. And it's stupid.

If you see the word "luxury," run for the hills. There is a whole economy designed to separate people from their money. And it's a con job. Do you need a Mercedes? No. Do you need a thousand-dollar bottle of wine? Hell, no. A private jet? Okay, maybe.

A private jet is worth it. It really is. They're a gazillion dollars, but you never have to go through airport security again! What a dream. I've been on them. They're amazing. They have movies and drawers filled with snacks. They even have a drawer underneath the seat that has even more snacks. And the seats are so comfortable and the planes are so fast. And the pilots are paid more so they're happier and look like they really enjoy their jobs and don't want to die.

Yeah, if you can get enough money for a private jet, you

should do it. Even if it means not having any money left over for anything else, it's well worth it. You'll live in a studio apartment, sleep on a futon, and eat Amy's frozen burritos. You'll wear clothes from Costco, the only jewelry you'll own is a bracelet your daughter made you, and you won't own a car. But who cares? You'll have a jet!

That would be a pretty great life.

The rest is a joke. The luxury hotel, the designer clothes, the luxury gym, the expensive seats at the stadium, it's all a lie. A watch for two hundred thousand dollars? You're nuts. College tuition for half a million dollars? Get lost.

And you know who you're surrounded by when you pay for a hotel room that costs two thousand a night and eat in restaurants serving thousand-dollar caviar? A lot of rich duds. They're no fun. No one plays music. No one has real conversations. They just walk around with labels on their goofy shirts and look at what labels you're wearing and talk about interest rates and taxes.

And they do annoying things, like they wear all-white outfits so they can go summer. I can't wear all white. If I wear a white shirt, I sweat through it in twenty minutes. It looks like I'm smuggling turkey gravy under my armpits.

And they summer. Do you summer? I don't summer. Summer happens and I deal with it.

Here's a secret that no one tells you. After all the money, and all the wealth, do you know what a lot of super-rich people are? They're bored. They are truly, undoubtedly bored. When you have so much money that you can do anything and you have already done everything, there's nothing left to do.

So why is this a goal? So you can make so much money that you end up isolated from everybody else? You go from your private helicopter to your private island to your mansion completely alone? What fun is that? We're only here once, you have to mix it up and get out there.

Look, I'm not Pollyannaish about it. Sometimes when I'm in a crowd of people I wish I had my own helicopter. Not just to escape: I fantasize about turning it upside down and chopping everybody's head off. But for the most part, people are pretty great.

We're all the same, no matter how much money you have in the bank. If you have friends, family, and community, something creative to do, and you are kind to people and create a world that you are happy to live in, then money is not that important. It truly isn't. If you have any of that, you are already rich.

But man, if you can, get a private jet!

HAVE YOU EVER GOTTEN TO THE END OF A WATERSLIDE AND HAD TO WAIT FOR YOUR SHORTS TO FLOAT TO THE SURFACE? I HAVE...

DON'T GO TUBING

We've all had those times when people make you feel like you're supposed to do something despite everything in your body telling you that you shouldn't do it. Things like jumping off the high dive, wearing Crocs, or slow dancing with your uncle at a wedding.

Sometimes doing the things that we think are beyond us is how we grow and become better, happier people. When you come back to the surface after finally making that jump, you feel pretty damn good about yourself. But then there are those things that are just plain stupid. Dumb-ass things that you really shouldn't do, despite everyone pressuring you into it.

Like tubing.

Have you ever gone tubing? It's when you sit in a giant inner tube and float down a river. A big, fat, stupid car or truck tire that you have no way to steer, no way to stop, and no way to control. It's really stupid.

People also use these inner tubes to fly down snow-filled mountains. Do you know what happens when you do that? You bounce. You bounce around a lot. And eventually, through momentum, you bounce right out of the inner tube into a fence.

That's what happened to a friend of mine, the great comedian Robert Kelly, while his young child looked on from down below and his wife filmed it on her phone. I saw my friend, my lovable, overweight friend, flying down the side of the mountain. He was going faster than anything else, scorching past snowboarders and skiers as if they were trees.

"Look at Daddy go," his wife said.

"Is he going too fast?" asked his frightened six-year-old son.

Yeah, that's right, kid, way too fast. People were running for their lives. Hopping away in ski boots, trying to get out of the path of this human avalanche.

Bobby should have slowed down or steered away from the children and old people going for hot cocoa. But he couldn't do any of those things because his ass was stuck in an inner tube.

There would be no slowing down. There would be no stopping. There would be only insane acceleration.

"Uh-oh," his wife said as he neared the bottom.

"I think he's going way too fast," his son said.

Bobby reached the end of the slope where the snow came to an end. The tube stopped. Time stopped. Bobby did not. He was launched like a rag doll in snow pants, up into the air, as if he'd been fired from a slingshot, smack into a fence.

He could have really been hurt. He could have died. It's one of the funniest things I have ever seen.

But he never should have done it.

I made a similar mistake in college, putting my own butt in an inner tube and heading out into roaring rapids in upstate New York. I didn't want to do it. It seemed like a dumb thing to do. But I caved in to the peer pressure from my friends and my girlfriend and found myself sitting on a school bus in my bathing suit. If you're in a bathing suit, you should be in a pool, the ocean, or maybe a lake. You shouldn't be on a school bus, even if that school bus is filled only with adults.

We were being driven deep into the woods by a man who looked like the kind of guy you don't want driving you into the woods. He was barefoot and had facial hair that either grew in patches or was nibbled away by the pet rat that was perched on his shoulder. He didn't say much, but when he did he punctuated it by spitting on the floor of the bus.

We all had to sign a form that absolved this man and his organization of anything bad that might happen to us, including death. A good way to live your life is to not do anything that requires you signing one of those forms. Anytime someone hands you a pen when you don't have time to read it or have a lawyer present, just put the pen down and walk away.

I've signed a whole bunch of these forms, right before I stepped onto a helicopter, joined a questionable snorkeling trip in Mexico, and was handed rented ski equipment. Sometimes I've even signed these forms as they took my children away to be strapped into a harness for something stupid like zip-lining.

I don't know why you would need to sign anything when you are tubing. No judge in the world is going to hold the tubing place liable for your dumb choice to go flying over waterfalls in a tire.

You also have to question how enjoyable an activity really is if you have to get drunk in the middle of it. Tubing is so stupid that you have to start drinking as soon as you agree to do it. I was in charge of getting the beer because in our weird-looking group I was the most normal-looking one and I wasn't.

I had long curly hair and a tie-dyed shirt, was pretty fat, and wore those Velcro sandals called Tevas that were popular for a couple of weeks in the 1990s. If I didn't look like one of Jesus's apostles, I did look like one of the apostles' fat friends.

We were drinking the entire way up, along treacherous country roads that the driver and his rat seemed to know pretty well. They really enjoyed going around turns as quickly as possible so that we would all fall off our seats, and be smooshed against the windows.

"Hang on," he'd say much too late.

As we got off the bus, it looked like the county jail had decided to give some of the hippie inmates a day in the country. The driver climbed up to the metal roof rack and started throwing inner tubes at us with a little too much glee.

As everyone was trying to pick up their tube while not spilling their beer, I asked our driver to direct us to a safe spot to enter the river. He just spit and started up the bus. His rat gave us the finger as they took off, leaving us in a cloud of parking lot dust.

We made our way to the water and started off splashing each other and gently drifting downstream as we got settled in. We had so much beer that it got its own inner tube. I held the rope attached to the beer tube like I was walking a dog.

The scenery was actually pleasant as the deep green summer trees were waving us on with their giant maple leaves and mighty oak branches. A friendly fish or two would swim up to say hello. I was with my girlfriend, surrounded by friends, and full of youth and sunshine. You might think that this sounds nice. That it sounds like a pretty good time. And it was. For about five minutes.

The first sign of trouble was when we picked up speed. Just a little faster, but fast enough that some in the group started to hoot. Whenever someone from your group starts to hoot, there's a good chance you're in trouble.

The only thing louder was the constant, growing roar we heard in the distance. This was the sound of a roaring river. This ancient body of water that has been cutting through the earth's crust for millions of years was being hurled to greater depths and smacking against rocks.

How did this group of college kids with brains swimming in beer think they were going to master this body of water? On inner tubes. No handles. No motors. Not even paddles. Even lame people in canoes have paddles. Maniacs in kayaks have a two-sided paddle. Retirees in leisure wear on paddleboats have paddles. We were dumber than all of them. We didn't have paddles. We had beer attached to a rope.

And the beer was now going faster than I was. Beer was apparently excited about the rapids. Beer was so excited that it was pulling me like a friend rushing to the stage at a concert.

The first rapids were like the little dips on a roller coaster. My friends were screaming, but they were fun, exaggerated screams as the river pulled us in our silly little tire boats quickly into itself and down between the rocks.

And it worked. Somehow we got through. Sure, we were spun around, and a couple of us ended up backward, but we made it. We all did. Even the beer seemed to be swimming up to everyone and trading a beer for a pat on its head. We felt invincible.

But now another roar began and it was more constant and ferocious than it was before. We fell silent. We were worried. We were concerned. We were screwed.

This was not cute anymore. We were about to find out why we signed that stupid form. Even the beer was turning around, trying to head back upstream.

My friend Chris, who was way ahead of us, was now really screaming and it was no longer that cute "ain't this fun" scream. This was a scream of horror. Something bad was happening to him up around the bend and he wanted us to know that we should be paddling in the other direction or at least steering ourselves into a better position. But again, we couldn't do any of that, because we were floating at the mercy of the river on a piece of rubber.

We were so deep in the canyon that there was no more sunlight. The temperature dropped, the roar was deafening, and this was no longer fun. This was a place that you went to only if you made a mistake or were on some kind of *Lord of the Rings* quest.

We were gaining speed. As Robert's child said in the video, we were now going "way too fast."

I don't remember much of it. I do remember seeing a nearby horizon line ahead of me where there shouldn't have been one. I wondered why that was and why I was suddenly even with the tops of giant pine trees. And then I realized that I had reached the edge and that I was about to drop to my death over the falls.

I also remember my girlfriend flying past and reaching out for me as if she were being tossed off a skyscraper. I was her only hope, but unlike Tom Cruise, I didn't even try and catch her. I just watched her go over the side.

I let go of the beer rope and tried to hold on to my tube, but it bounced me out of it as if it, too, were scared and didn't need me messing with its chances. And then I dropped over the side of the falls like a stone, like a drunk, tubeless, Teva-kicking, beer-filled stone. I was immediately underwater and, as if someone were spraying me with a fire hose, was pushed deeper and deeper below the surface by this angry waterfall.

Have you ever been knocked over by a powerful wave and had no idea what your body was doing or which way was up or if there even was an up anymore? At a certain point you just surrender. You might come out of it. You might die. But you don't really care anymore. That was me, but instead of being in a rock-free sandy ocean, I was in a rock-filled river. And that was exactly what I hit, a giant rock, at the bottom of the river, first with my head and then with my entire body.

I was like a wet leaf folding over the shape of the rock. My arms and legs were spread-eagled and I was stuck, pinned by centuries of momentum, and I was losing breath and I was hurt and pretty sure I was going to die. Die from tubing. What a horrible thing for everybody to have to try and say, without laughing, at my funeral.

For a split second it actually became very peaceful. But then nature took over, as nature always does, and it pushed me loose. I was off the rock and back into the frantic washing machine, but now I saw light. It was the sun and I was rising. But I didn't feel like it was calling to me as much as laughing at me. Laughing at this chubby, curly-haired dude who thought the river was a joke.

I burst to the surface like a man taking his first breath. My girlfriend, who had skittered across the top of the rapids like a dainty flower, unscathed, raised her hands in triumph because her fat boyfriend was alive. My other friends cheered and said things like "Man, that was awesome," and "We thought you were dead."

It wasn't awesome. Breaking a couple of ribs on a rock at the bottom of a waterfall is stupid. It was also stupid that I had no choice but to get back on my tube and continue on because there was no other way out.

Would I do it again? Hell, no. Because we don't have to do everything. There are some things that you should be proud that you skipped, that you said no to. And if you're confused about what those dumb things are, just remember to look for the form.

A LOT HAS CHANGED

When we were dating, my wife and I shared an apartment that had a bedroom in the back overlooking a tiny alleyway where pigeons would get stuck and peck each other to death. That's where we fell in love.

It was in Chelsea, on West Twenty-first Street between Eighth and Ninth in New York City, just at the time when the gay community showed up, looked around, and decided things should be fixed up a bit. We wouldn't have been able to afford it if she hadn't lived there for years with an ever-rotating array of roommates under a questionable lease.

She had to pretend her name was Jen, keep a stranger's last name on the mailbox, and if anything went wrong in the apartment, we would have to fix it ourselves rather than call the superintendent and have him snooping around for the landlord.

When I moved in we were able to share the rent, which made things a lot easier. A lot of relationships go the next step in New York simply because of housing. I used to say that I fell in love with her the minute I saw her place.

I loved the apartment and hated it at the same time. All

New York apartments have their quirks. This one was extremely narrow, like a hallway with rooms, but when you're young you don't really care if it's imperfect because you're continually surprised and proud that you're actually able to live in this monstrous metropolis.

The first thing I did when I moved in was to knock down the loft bed in the bedroom. A loft bed, for those of you who live in normal places, is like a bunk bed with only the top bunk. They're popular in city apartments because they allow you to use the space underneath for a desk, a yoga studio, or more likely a bike that you hang your laundry on. The problem with this loft was that it was built too high and left only about six inches between the bed and the ceiling, so anytime I rolled over I would smash my face into it. Sex was out of the question, unless your idea of a good time was making love in an MRI machine.

I used the bumps on my head to plead my case that we had to knock it down. I was proud and relieved when I finally hauled all the wood out of the apartment and left it on the sidewalk. This is what you do with anything you need to get rid of in New York. Wood, bottles, bodies can all be placed on the sidewalk, where eventually someone else will take it away. I really enjoyed putting out books, old records, or clothes and watching from the window as strangers picked through and judged everything we owned.

No one would ever tell you that the shirt you were wearing was ugly, but when they're holding it up on the street it's a different thing entirely. I once watched as the local homeless guy who wore the same tattered clothes every day held up a jacket of mine, laughed, shook his head, and put it back.

The responses to books were great, too. I loved watching judgmental New Yorkers hold a Grisham book in their hand, stare up at the building as if they were trying to figure out what simpleton ever thought this was good, and then sneak it into their grocery bag and walk off.

Back in the apartment we swept out the room and put the bed down at floor level. The only problem with this was that we were now able to see out the window. It was a smaller than normal window, in a smaller than normal bedroom, in this smaller than normal apartment. I'm not sure why there was even a window there. It didn't look out on anything but an alley about the size of a pizza box, between three other buildings.

It really served no purpose other than as a prison for pigeons that mistakenly got caught in there. They must have gotten caught in some kind of draft that pushed them down into it and prevented them from flying out. At times there could be as many as ten stuck down there in this bird purgatory.

Unable to fly, they stood around on the bottom, confused and teased by the sunlight shining in from up above. There was always a lot of noisy cooing, as if they were discussing their predicament. I imagined an older pigeon who had been down there for a while, spitting a piece of concrete out of his beak and telling the new arrivals how it worked down there. "There ain't no use trying to fly. No one ever gets out of the hole."

After a while they would all go mad and out of hunger or anger would pick out the weakest bird and peck it to death. I don't know if they ate it, I never stuck around that long, but I did see them all join together in a circle and with their beaks destroy another pigeon like a biker gang at Altamont.

All we could do was close the curtain, crawl back onto the bed, and go to sleep.

During the winter months we'd keep the window closed and pretend nothing was out there, but during the hot and humid summers, when we actually put an air conditioner in that window, the pigeons and us became roommates.

We were just as desperate as those birds and risked breathing in whatever diseases their feathers carried past the filter and into our room. We didn't care. Unlike a lot of people in that building, and many of our friends, we finally had cold air. We were Air-Conditioner People.

Looking back, I admit life in that apartment seems intolerable, but we were young, in love, and making it work. We were hardly inside anyway, which is why the streets of New York are always crowded: everyone wants out of their apartments.

The neighborhood was great. There was the great Bendix Diner on the corner of West Twenty-first and Eighth Avenue. It was a healthy but hearty twist on a regular diner, way before that was a thing. And unlike the "cool" places today, the Bendix didn't make you endure the indignity of standing in line as if it were a bread line, ordering by yourself, and walking off with a number that you placed on a table you had to fight for. This was back in a time when restaurants had hostesses and waiters. It was quite a thing.

Across the street was a great Mexican place run by a creative woman who spent a lot of her time traveling throughout Mexico collecting recipes and ingredients that she would bring back and share with us. To this day I haven't found a burrito as perfectly delicious as those.

On the other side of Twenty-first was a gay bar named Rawhide. The neighborhood was more gay than straight, with gay coffee shops, sex shops, and the Chinese restaurant that wasn't gay but had the biggest rainbow flag in the city. At times it felt like we were the only hetero couple around, which I always enjoyed. It somehow made us more exotic.

My favorite place was the Gamin Café. It was a French bistro on West Twenty-first and Ninth and was the perfect place to write and drink great coffee. I loved it there. They never made you feel that you had to eat something or give up your table and move along. They were happy to have you, and while this may sound obnoxious, I think they liked us there because we were real writers, unlike those people setting up offices at Starbucks only to return emails. Whenever I see too many other people around with their laptops open I suspect there's more shopping and Facebook than work.

But at Gamin, most of the time, there was only one other person working and there were no laptops, just quiet, respectful pen and paper. I wrote in, and still write in, Mead Cambridge 8½-by-11-inch college-ruled pads with the spiral on the top so the pages flip up and over rather than side to side like a book.

The great thing about writing in a notebook is that it's just for writing. It doesn't have the multifaceted utility that a laptop has. With the pad there will be no emails to read, no weather forecasts to check, and no quick looks at the internet to see what celebrity gossip you're missing. The only important thing is what you're writing. Or not.

I'd grab my notebook, kiss my wife, head down to Gamin, order their dark, rich coffee, and start. It was heaven. The waiters all spoke French or English with French accents. Everything was perfectly bistro, from the wicker chairs to the tin walls and unhurried pace. I'd laugh when new patrons would come in and complain about the slow service as if this were a problem and not the whole point.

If nothing was happening with my writing, rather than fill that nothing space with technology I'd sit and watch the cook making breakfast or the waitress flirting at the opposite table. I could eavesdrop on the conversation between the two novelists going on about their weekend upstate or drink another cup of coffee, look out the window, and let New York handle the storytelling.

On really good days I could write in there for hours, just long enough to get hungry. Cynthia would come down, and I'd put the notebook away and make room for the perfect crepes, croque madame, and toasted baguette with the best butter in the world and somehow when it rained everything tasted even better.

As happens in New York, we stayed in that apartment longer than we probably should have, but we loved it and we loved each other, and even if we wanted to leave, our roots were growing deeper.

We made love and planned for our future there. We celebrated life and dealt with death there. We got engaged and married and returned there to spend the night of our wedding.

In the weeks and months after 9/11, we hosted friends and family as we tried to piece our world back together. We regained hope there and decided in the wake of that tragic event to make a family. And we brought our first baby home from the hospital by taxi and sat on the front steps of the apartment on Father's Day, proud that we followed through on our promise to bring more good people into the world.

We converted the apartment for her and filled it with all the things that a baby needs: cribs, strollers, and mountains of plastic toys that eventually took over our lives and started to tell us that it was time to leave. But still we stayed.

Even when we had to move to Los Angeles for a while, we couldn't let the apartment go, renting it out to friends and family who all had to adopt the secret identity of Jen to keep the place going.

When we became a family of four and moved back, we knew we couldn't push the walls of that tiny hallway of a place any further. The kids only remember playing with their grandparents, dancing on the sidewalk, and jumping through the snow that turned the street into their magical playground. But we knew it was time to go.

The neighborhood has changed a lot. We go by when we can, and my wife is always shocked when a business has closed or a restaurant has become something new.

"Oh my God," she'll say, "look at that, Kelly's is gone. Oh no."

She sees every business closing as a small but significant death, and she's not wrong. Bendix is gone, the gay coffee shop is gone, even Rawhide has been shuttered, which would be fine if they weren't all replaced with banks and nail salons. We're not alone in thinking that New York, especially Manhattan, has been taken over by big business and we're quickly losing what made it a neighborhood worth living in.

But New York goes through cycles, and there are signs that small-city living will remain. The Laundromat is still there and the school across the street is still alive and filled with new students every year. And Gamin is still going strong, even though it's changed its name.

Last fall we walked by our old apartment and the first-floor window, our window, was decorated for Halloween. We joked that they weren't doing it right and criticized the window dressing as if the apartment still belonged to us, and in a very real way it still does.

We like to picture some young couple inside, loving it and hating it and starting off their life together just as we did. I hope they're as hopeful and carefree as we were, despite having to sleep in that back room to the sounds of those spooky pigeons. Or better yet, I hope that all those birds figured a way to get out and finally flew away.

A SIMPLE CUP OF COFFEE

There was a time when I thought that the most important thing in life was sex. Then I thought the most important thing in life was money. Now I realize that the most important thing in life is coffee.

Java. Joe. Dirt. Mud. Cupped lightning. Whatever you call it, it's damn good and without it I'm not sure that I would get through a day without killing someone.

I really do love it. I love it here, I love it there, even when I'm in my underwear. I love it at home or wherever I am. I even love it with green eggs and ham.

I go to sleep at night with a smile on my face because I know that the next time I open my eyes I'm getting another cup of coffee. The first cup of the day, which may be the greatest. Everything comes alive. As soon as that deep aromatic smell hits my brain, my entire being knows the day is about to improve. Whatever happened in that bed last night, no matter what evil monsters visited me in my dreams, despite how many times I got up to pee, coffee is the reset button and all that is wrong will once again be right.

When I'm home I have several methods that I've perfected for the creation of this mighty drink. Each of these options is designed for a single cup, which is all I need in my house, as I'm the only coffee drinker. The women I live with seem to be living a very different life under the same roof. They don't like coffee, eat meat, smoke cigars, or listen to John Coltrane. Those are moments I enjoy on my own, unless I'm grilling a steak, in which case I'm joined by a very enthusiastic dog.

My first method is a small Nespresso machine that makes a solid espresso in as little as thirty seconds. It's a reliable device that really does the trick, especially when I have only enough time for a single shot and a quick slice of sourdough toast. I also like that it has an Italian-sounding name. For a kid from New Jersey, it makes me feel like I'm doing something European, which must be right.

When I have more time, I prefer the slower but more satisfying single-cup pour-over method. It takes extra steps, but those steps are almost as enjoyable as drinking it. First you get to put a pot of water on the stove and boil it. There's something about the timelessness of the fire, the pot, and the time that has a real primal effect on me. They didn't use a Nepresso or Keurig pods in ancient Greece, but there has always been fire and a metal pot.

While that boils, I move on to grinding the coffee beans, which creates an aroma that's so deep and rich, I've thought about putting a little behind my ears like a fine cologne.

When the beans have been ground, I pour them into a cone device with a metal filter that sits on the coffee cup, and the pour-over begins. It's like filling a funnel, in that you can do only so much at a time as the water heads down over the beans and into the cup.

This takes probably four to five minutes in total, much longer than the instant coffee machines, but like all things in life that take a little more time, it is much sweeter. The flavor is fuller and echoes over the back of your tongue for minutes afterward, letting you savor the coffee and the wise choice you made to slow down and truly enjoy yourself.

I'm aware that I'm getting a little carried away here, but it's the taking notice of these small, attainable things in life that cuts down on the malaise. It creates a memorable experience out of the mundane. Coffee is like wine for people playing it straight.

I also have a Keurig machine that brews larger American-size cups. I bought this one for when my father visits. The European size of the smaller machine doesn't satisfy his American habit. He refers to the smaller cups as "Girl Scout size."

The Keurig makes what he calls "a normal cup of coffee." He buys the strongest stuff he can find, with names like Double Black Diamond, Hair Raiser, and Coal Mine Sludge. He's not looking for anything fancy. He wants it hot. He wants it black. And he wants it fast.

My mother reported that recently he's been waking up in the middle of the night, walking into the kitchen, drinking a cup of coffee, and returning straight back to bed. It helps him sleep. For most people this would have the opposite effect, but he's really not like the rest of us.

He doesn't understand this fancy coffee craze either. He comes from the 1960s and 1970s, also known as the Great American Coffee Depression. They had some really bad coffee back there. I'm not sure how they survived. They had only two options: Thick & Black or Watery & Sad. Everything came in Styrofoam cups or, when they were entertaining, those paper cups with the cardboard handles on the side.

There were no coffee shops back then. The closest they came to a coffee shop was a doughnut shop, but let's be honest, that wasn't about the coffee. You're not thinking about coffee when you are scratching your tummy, trying to decide between a jelly doughnut and a bear claw.

They got their coffee in places like muffler shops, hardware stores, and police stations. People back then hoped to be called for jury duty because they knew there'd be coffee there with names like Sanka, Maxwell House, and Chock full o'Nuts. It came in big cans and was scooped into machines with names like Mr. Coffee that were sold by retired baseball players.

This was a time when coffee was made by the pot.

"I'm making a pot."

"Will you stay awhile? I'm going to make us a pot."

An uncle would walk into the house drunk, yelling about the government, and my mother would help him to a seat in the kitchen and say, "You sit right there, I'm going to put on a pot."

To this day, my sister uses an old-fashioned percolator from this era. She inherited it from my grandmother. It's a big metal pitcher with a closed top. It plugs into the wall and takes some time, but it brews great coffee, made better because it's been with us for so long.

I remember running around on my childish adventures while the grandparents, aunts, uncles, and parents would sit together in the living room. This was the final stage of yet another family get-together. The holiday meal was over. Everyone was a little drowsy from the food and from the alcohol that they never drank much of, just enough to put a haze over the end of the afternoon. The dishes were done, the drying complete.

The conversation at this point was pleasant and subdued. Any political arguments or stinging gossip from earlier in the day had run its course. All the hustle, traffic, and familial anxiety, was over. Everyone had gotten through it and together realized it wasn't all that bad.

For this final hour, with belts loosened and hair let down, there was no worry about the past or what was to come. The soft laughter and calm were as pure and suspended as the setting sun, enveloped by the sound and smell of the trusty percolator.

That all these years later that percolator continues to brew as we sit in some of the same chairs, experiencing the same feelings and telling stories about all of them, makes for a special cup of coffee. Everything is better with a story.

But how lucky are we that we're alive during the American Coffee Revolution. We've got great coffee everywhere we go. We have more coffee shops than we have people.

Complaints about corporate behemoths aside, Starbucks really nailed it and led the way. The dark coffee-bean wood. The natural green. The smell of the beans that fills the shop. The right level of music. A place to sit. And it's not a mistake that they sell real old-fashioned newspapers. This has all been thought out or rather tailored to the things that coffee drinkers, real coffee drinkers, enjoy but had been missing, and they inspired thousands of other shops to do it in their own style.

We have so many options now. Small independent coffee shops, Barnes & Noble Starbucks mash-ups, free trade coffee, coffee pods, Illy, coffee and cake, coffee and pie, diner coffee, coffee bean, Seattle's Best. Even the Dunkin' Donuts people have been making some noise, but the colors of their shop alone annoy me. It looks like a ten-year-old girl's cupcake party. How can I enjoy a good cup of coffee in a shop that was designed by Hello Kitty?

Entire regions are based on coffee. The Pacific Northwest is coffee crazy. There are espresso shops on every corner and long winding country roads. Shops that match the rhythm of what you want out of an espresso, with coffee so dark and stormy it's as if it dropped right out of an overcast Seattle sky.

Portland is another great coffee town. New York's West Village cafés, Silver Lake independent roasters, Austin, Chicago, and Minneapolis. There seems to be a direct correlation between the number of rainy days and the number of great coffee shops in a city. Sorry, Miami.

And I'm sorry, Canada, but Tim Hortons stinks. (This may have to come out if I ever want to tour in Canada again.)

Is it an addiction? You bet it is. Do I like being addicted? You bet I do. Some addictions are pretty great. Just reading the word gets me excited for another cup. Did I just do that to you? I hope so.

Coffee has been around all this time because it works and it is cherished. Think of all those coffee moments in the movies when someone orders a cup of Joe. When a waitress slides the coffee across the counter to a weary traveler. A cowboy holding a cup of coffee at the early-morning fire. The soldier on the edge of battle drinking a cup and restoring something normal in his life.

Coffee is good. Coffee is to be enjoyed. Coffee is one of those reliable things that can make the world better.

So what do you say? Want to come up for some coffee? I'll put on a pot.

HAVE YOU EVER TAKEN A BREAK WHILE HIKING AND SAT ON A LOG FILLED WITH FIRE ANTS? MY WIFE HAS . . .

STAY INSIDE WHERE YOU'RE SAFE

I've been attacked by animals my entire life. It's not that I'm looking for a fight. I'm actually a big fan of nature and its inhabitants, but for some reason they really want to bite me.

Just this morning I had a squirrel throw a nut at me. A squirrel's entire existence is finding and saving nuts. It's pretty much their only job. And yet this squirrel took one look at me sipping my coffee on the back patio, hauled off, and threw it at my head.

I know on a global scale humans are killing off a lot of the animals and leaving a barren planet in our wake. There isn't a nature documentary that doesn't end with sad music, smokestacks, and Morgan Freeman telling us how awful mankind is. But from where I'm standing, the animals aren't so great either.

And I'm not in Montana or in some national park; I'm staying at my sister's house in New Jersey. When you hear "New Jersey," wildlife isn't the first thing that comes to mind. But trust me, they're here and they're just as mean and bullying as everyone else in New Jersey.

There's a fat mourning dove sitting under the eave of the roof off the kitchen. Apparently it's been there for weeks. There's suspicion that she's sitting on an egg and waiting for it to hatch. I went out to look at it and another bird, probably her boyfriend, flew at my head as a warning shot. The mama bird gave me a dismissive look. The squirrel laughed from the fence.

Birds have been attacking me for years. When I was in third grade we moved to a new house. It was exciting, and on moving day, as my parents were doing all the moving, I was running around exploring the house. I was checking out all the important spots: my new room, the backyard, and more important where I'd be watching nonstop TV. I was running, jumping, and filled with joy. And then I went into the basement.

Basements are always a little scary. Something about going down, underneath the life of the house, gives one pause. You can be in the nicest house there is, filled with love and fresh-baked cookies, and you open that basement door, start walking down the stairs, and your heart skips a beat. There's a reason scary movies don't take place in the kitchen: that's not where the evil is—that's in the basement.

What made this even scarier was that this wasn't some fancy finished basement with carpeted stairs. This was a cellar. A dingy, musty-smelling cellar where they bury the bodies and the bad guys tie the good guy to a chair and torture him for information. Where Satan himself would patiently wait among skulls and demons for you to visit on the first day in your new house.

I took a deep breath and headed down. Each creaky step was speaking to me in a new way, in a much different language from that of the stairs in my old home. It was unclear what they were saying, but it seemed to have something to do with death.

When I finally got to the bottom I thought I was safe. The fear subsided. It was just a basement. It wasn't so bad. And then, out of the corner of my eye I saw something move. Something black moving across the ceiling. The kind of image that you think might be a shadow or something in your eyelash. But then it turned and came back in the other direction, letting out a screeching, unholy scream.

Holy demonballs!

It thrashed back and forth across the room. Shrieking in a foreign tongue that it was going to kill me by eating my face and working its way down to my sneakers. I couldn't move. All I could do was watch as it turned and came for me, hitting me square in the chest. I wet my pants.

I turned and started to run, or rather I tried to run, tried my best to get back up those steps. But I was falling and shaking and screaming a silent scream that would not come out of my mouth. My legs were useless, so I tried pulling myself up by my arms instead. I lost a shoe. I slid back down. I lost the other shoe. The beast cackled and picked up speed.

Frantically scrambling on all fours, fueled by terror, I made my way to the top of this hellish place.

My parents found me in a heap, one sock missing, the other hanging off my foot like a worm. My father yelled at me to stop crying. All I could do was point to the underworld like that kid in *The Shining* after he met those twin girls.

My father went downstairs, thinking I was ridiculous, and within a second there was another shriek. The beast was upon him.

"Holy shit!" he said. "It's a crow. A gigantic crow!"

He was right. A giant black crow was trying to escape through closed windows. Its wings, its evil feet, and its murderous face all joined together in hell's fury and was attacking my father.

I passed out.

This is how it goes with the animals and me. Most people would see a friendly wren or a cartoon hummingbird carrying a flower in its beak. I was visited by a death bird, normally found on top of a gravestone or sitting on Edgar Allan Poe's shoulder.

I've had a seagull take a crap on me at a wedding, a hawk take a piece of chicken off my plate, and some kamikaze bird fly into my helmet when I was taking my motorcycle test. And when they're not attacking it's only because they're watching me from telephone wires and through open windows, devising their next plan.

It's not just birds. It's all sorts of animals. As a small child I was sitting in our living room, peacefully playing with my Hot Wheels, when out of nowhere, like an attack from above, a raccoon fell down the chimney and landed with a thud into the fireplace. He was scared. I was shocked. We both started screaming.

The thing you have to know about raccoons is that they have human hands and are smarter than most teenagers. As I stood there in shock, holding two toy cars, he slowly climbed over the fireplace fence. His eyes were staring me down, telling me not to say a word, and when he knew he was in control, he took off into the kitchen.

When you hear your mother screaming for her life in another room, you worry about her. When you see her run past you in the living room and out the front door, you worry about yourself. When she pokes her head back in the door and yells for you to run, you do as you're told.

I ran outside and she slammed the front door closed, locking the raccoon inside. "The cookies!" my mother yelled.

"Nooooo," I cried.

Slowly, we went back inside and thankfully the raccoon was

gone and the cookies were untouched. Had he used his human hands to climb back up the fireplace? We were confused, but we were safe. We hugged and laughed and just as I reached for a cookie, he jumped off the top cabinet like a ninja and slammed onto the tray. My mother screamed. The raccoon screamed.

I wet my pants.

Eventually my mother got him out of the house with a broom, and without thinking that we might contract rabies, we ate the cookies and drank some milk.

I'm surprised I never got a disease from all these animal encounters. There was ample opportunity to come down with something. It seems like every other person I know has Lyme disease. The entire East Coast is crawling with deer ticks that burrow through your skin and into your bloodstream just because you dared to leave your house.

A tick is smaller than a sesame seed. Not a sesame-seed bagel, a single seed. And you have to check yourself every time you come back inside to make sure that you don't have one digging through your skin and swimming around through your bloodstream for all of eternity. Enjoy your hike.

You might get lucky and have the bull's-eye-shaped rash on your body, which is how your body reacts when a tick decides to live inside you. It's a red ring with a bull's-eye center. But if you don't get lucky and detect it early enough, you'll end up with Lyme disease, lose all your energy and your mind. That's fun.

The deer in New Jersey, who carry the ticks on their bodies like jewelry, are staging their own takeover. They're everywhere. Driving around my sister's neighborhood is like going through some weird animal haunted house where deer pop out from behind every tree.

I don't have a great history with these creatures either. I

was attacked by a deer at a wedding when I was younger. (See Book I.) My girlfriend and I hit a deer with her car, and for years they would charge at us as if the rest of the herd hadn't forgotten about it.

There's no way around it, the animals hate me. I've been bit by a crab on my crotch and stung in the face by a jellyfish. I had a moose chase me down a hiking trail because I came too close to its daughter. I once woke up with a cockroach in my mouth. I've been stung by bees and wasps and bitten by spiders all in the same day. I wouldn't be surprised to come out of my house in the morning to find a group of wild dogs stealing my car.

The lesson I've learned from all these attacks is that we shouldn't underestimate the animals. Nature is tough to stop. Even in New York City. Pigeons are an unstoppable force, ducks and seagulls are all over the parks. And of course there's the main animal, the one that occupies even more space than all the people in all the buildings: the rats.

Rats are everywhere.

No one is making a documentary about the rats with the sad final scene of the humans doing them in. That's not happening. The rats are dominant. The rats are growing. The rats will outlast us. The polar bears would do well to spend some time with the rats.

They're everywhere. Every restaurant in New York has a rating on its window, a letter grade that tells customers how clean they are. All those letters really show is how the owners are doing in their battle to the death versus the rats.

They ride the subway, they eat in cafés, they crap on sidewalks and in utensil drawers. They work alone, they work in pairs, and they roam the streets in gangs. They are the ultimate recyclers. There's no such thing as garbage to a rat. Nothing goes to waste when the rats come to town.

I've seen entire streets that at first glance seem to be moving, that were really just covered with rats. My wife walked by the iconic New York Public Library steps where the proud lion statues sit out front, covered with rats. It was as if the rats were letting everyone know that in this urban jungle there was a very different king.

We are the visitors. The animal kingdom ain't no joke. And what about germs? Are we counting germs? Those microscopic beings who are quietly getting stronger and fighting off all the antibiotics we can come up with? Flu bugs, allergy bugs, they're everywhere, and all the antiseptic hand washes and antibacterial lotions are just pushing them to the side for a moment. They float in the air, dance on handrails, and fly right up your nose.

As far as I'm concerned, the animals win. I give up. And you should, too. Let's make a deal. If they want the outdoors, they can have it. We'll stay inside the air-conditioned safety of a restaurant and watch them through the window as long as they agree to stay out there.

But I don't trust they will.

SOMEONE TO LOVE

You need someone to love. Someone. Anyone. It doesn't even have to be a human being. It could be an animal. You just need two eyes looking at you from across the room. It could be a fish. A fish, just looking at you, one eye at a time. It makes you feel needed. It makes you accountable. It makes you feel loved.

If you do want a human being and you don't have one, it's your fault. You're being too picky. Your expectations are too high. There are seven billion people out there. You can find one. One. Are they perfect? Are they amazing? No. No one is. Which will make it easier to find the one person who doesn't make you throw up when they take their top off.

We're all somewhat unpleasant—which is another way of saying disgusting—and we're all flawed. All of us. That's what love is. Finding someone whose flaws you can put up with.

Have you ever taken the first flight out in the morning? That 6:00 A.M. flight, when you wake up at 4:00 and before you know it you are standing at security under fluorescent lights and you don't even know how you got there? You're not in control of your body and no one else is either. Everyone is shuffling along, confused, with their hair sticking up, wondering if they remembered to brush their teeth.

I love that moment. Because it's a sea of people you could have woken up with if you had made the wrong choice. I was on line recently behind this older gentleman who burped, farted, and sneezed all at the same time. He just exploded, out of all his openings, all at once, like a human tugboat.

It was horrible. People scattered. Changed lines. Changed flights. Went home and tried again tomorrow. His wife stood right next to him and did not flinch. She just scratched his back as if nothing had happened. She probably does the same thing. The two of them firing off every morning while they're making the coffee. The whole family probably does it. The cats, the dog, just popping off like the grand finale on the Fourth of July.

But they found each other. That's love.

Now, there's a good chance that the first time he erupted in front of her she might have thought it a little curious. "Huh, that's different." But her desire to have someone to eat cereal and toast with was greater than her repulsion about his gaseous habit. She did what everyone has to do while looking for love— she lowered her expectations.

They say don't judge a book by its cover. I say don't judge a book by its cover, its table of contents, or the first couple of chapters (this one included). You have to sit with a book for a long time. You have to live with it and take your time. You have to reread the parts that you read while you were distracted by thoughts of what to make for dinner and that thing the guy said at the supermarket.

Sometimes I will read the same chapter over and over and over and have no idea what's happening. I have books all over my office, on the shelves in the hallway, on my end table, and on a shelf in my bedroom, most written by some heavy hitters. Updike, Morrison, Twain, Steinbeck, Angelou. I have read them all. I see their bindings, the creases that I put there by flipping and reading every page. I'm not saying this to sound like an impressive reader, because truth be told, if I had to hand in a book report on any one of them, I would fail miserably.

But despite my retention, I loved reading them all. Those moments when I'm not thinking about the rest of my life and the words are the only thing that I'm focusing on, when they are focusing on me, I am at peace. Joyful peace.

I may not remember the names of all the family members in *East of Eden*, but I know that in my subconscious, they are there. Not up here on the surface, not accessible at the moment, but a part of me.

And people are the same. Something attracted you in the first place. There was some little piece of them that turned you on. And that should be enough. Don't start looking for negatives right away. Buy the book and give it a chance.

You need a lover.

A lover is the one person in the world who wants to hear about your travel day. The one person who really wants to know what you're thinking. The one person, in the whole world, who is truly worried when you feel like you're getting a cold.

They are the ones who will listen to you snore, watch you stick in a retainer and put on a sleep mask, and still think you're cute. They'll put sunscreen on your back without complaining, get you a glass of water, and truly look forward to you coming home.

They are there to listen to it all. All the stuff that you wouldn't waste people's time with at a cocktail party but that you have to get off your chest. No one wants to hear about every detail of your existence, every bug bite, and how you slept last night. That's stuff you share with your lover.

It's also about having someone to share a meal with. A plate of cheese with fresh bread and wine is a great thing on the worst of days; add another person and it's miraculous. It's an act of fulfillment and nourishment that is stronger and tastes better when it's with another human being.

And getting the focus off of us is important, too. It's good to have to think about someone else. We're not all that important. We think we are, but we're really not.

When you are living with someone else, your mind is on them just as much as it is on you. You hear the shower turn on and your focus is on them and how long that will take and where they're going.

I am in tune with everything my wife does. She carries an energy that I have come to know in a way that doesn't allow me to overthink my own. I know what her day is going to be like just by the way she comes out of the bedroom.

I know from how she opens the bedroom door what kind of day she has planned. If she has shoes on and stomps down the hallway with a quick step, she's not going to be here for long. She'll shorten her morning routine, say good morning to the cat from the stairs, and head out the door with determination. She won't get far. She never leaves just once. She'll forget something—she always forgets something—and will come back in for her keys, her water bottle, or her earbuds.

Or if I hear her come slowly out of her room and slowly down the hall, this is a day she doesn't have to be anywhere anytime soon. She'll stop at the laundry room, where the cat sleeps, she'll whisper good morning, opening the sliding wooden cat door, possibly open the washing machine door and turn on the water.

She'll head upstairs and wake up the dog, who's been asleep the entire time I've been in my office talking to you. She greets the dog the same way every time: "Oh boy. Look at you. Look at you."

With the animals taken care of, she'll stop by my door and give a report of how she slept or, more pointedly, how I slept. "I couldn't sleep at all last night. I fell asleep at first, but you snored all night. How many times did you get up to pee? Why did you get up so early?"

She'll head into the kitchen, turn on the lights, fill the teakettle with water, and take the coffee cup out of the cabinet. She'll empty the dishwasher, banging glasses and dishes into the cabinets. It's always loud, but I don't complain, as it's one of those jobs that she doesn't mind doing and that I would rather not.

I'll hear the dog bowl being filled with water and the food being poured from the bag. The teakettle going off, tea being poured, the newspaper freed from its bag, the stool slid out and sat on. Morning routine complete.

Eventually I'll come in to grab another cup of coffee and there will be those two eyes, looking at me from across the room.

"Where are you going?" she'll ask.

"What do you mean?"

"I know you're going out, I heard your keys."

HAVE YOU EVER SHOWN
YOUR CHILDREN A
FAVORITE COMEDY
FROM YOUR CHILDHOOD
AND REALIZED IT WAS
MISOGYNIST, CULTURALLY
TONE-DEAF, AND RACIALLY
INAPPROPRIATE? I HAVE . . .
(*REVENGE OF THE NERDS*)

THE GOOD OLD DAYS THAT WEREN'T

Lately you hear a lot of people pining for the good old days. A desire to return to the past, when life was simple, carefree, and just plain better. That's insane. The good old days didn't exist, it's a myth. We are so much luckier to be alive today. They didn't know how to do anything back then. We're just starting to figure out how to do stuff now and we're still not that good at it.

Have you ever seen the first bicycle ever built? I don't know a lot about building things, but I know you don't take the smallest wheel you can find and put that on the back and the biggest wheel on the planet and put that up front. That's a bad bike.

You couldn't even climb into the seat by yourself. You had to have your friends fling you up by the edges of your handlebar mustache and hope you landed on the seat. And once you started pedaling you couldn't stop, you had to pedal until you died, which was okay because your life expectancy back then was twenty-eight.

Their hospitals were horrible. All they knew how to do was cut your leg off. It didn't matter if you had a sore throat, acne, or a broken arm. You walked in and hopped right back out.

There was no birth control, no cortisone cream, no Advil.

Can you imagine a life without Advil? That doesn't sound like the good old days to me. Sometimes I open the cabinet looking for an Advil and discover that we've run out, and I just lie on the ground and pray for death. What else am I going to do, take that twelve-year-old Benadryl from its decaying package?

They didn't even have Tums. You just ate, got gassy, and exploded like a salami-filled piñata.

Things are much better now. Just look at all our beautiful fabrics and outfits. And you don't have just one pair of clothes, you have a whole array. Not in the good old days. Everyone had one stiff woolen suit and a pair of hard high-heeled dress shoes made out of pig livers. And they wore burlap underpants. Can you imagine? Have you ever wondered why no one ever smiled in those old black-and-white photographs? Now you know—burlap underpants.

The good old days didn't even have plumbing. You did your business in an outhouse, which wasn't a house at all. It was some planks gathered around a hole in the ground and your toilet paper was a stick. Some of my worst days were when we ran out of toilet paper and had to use napkins for a week. Can you imagine wiping yourself with a stick with poison ivy on the end?

Forget a nice hot shower, all you got in the GODs was a pickle barrel. That's how you got clean. Once every two weeks you took a bath in a pickle barrel, in the middle of the kitchen, with your entire family. Can you imagine? Can you imagine having to go last?! You'd dip in a pickle barrel filled with hair and grandma water, put on your burlap underpants, get on your dumb bike, and head to town.

You can keep the GODs, thank you very much. They didn't know nuthin'.

People were confused even as recently as the end of the twentieth century. Look at their cars. They were death traps made out of stupid metal and glass, filled with leaded gasoline, and no seat belts. No wonder people were drinking and driving so much, they were scared out of their minds.

The hospitals were still a mess. When I was born, my head was so big that it got stuck during childbirth. It's the same-size head I have now, on a tiny infant's body. Their solution was to take out a pair of rusty pliers used for carrying blocks of ice, grab my head, and pull. I don't care what line of work you're in, but you know you're dealing with idiots if their only solution is to "give it a pull."

They pulled. And they slipped. And slashed my little baby face from my chin to my temples on both sides. That was my introduction to the world: being dragged out by idiots and slashed across the face.

They were morons. Now I have a scar on my right cheek, like the Frankenstein monster, and my fate has been sealed—I'm now forced to wander the countryside alone, misunderstood, and chased by villagers with torches.

This was around the same time that they stopped an entire generation of infants from breastfeeding. The God-given way that human beings have survived and thrived was replaced by stripping babies from their mothers and giving them formula.

How did this turn out? Not great. Those same infants are now in control of Congress and the Senate. They have no empathy at all and don't seem that bright. And then they took away their fruits and vegetables and raised them on Pop-Tarts and Hawaiian Punch. You wonder why they don't care about global warming? Because they don't know that the earth is where food comes from. The closest to farming that they understand is when the Keebler Elves take the cookies out of the tree.

Good old days? They dumped toxic waste in rivers and oceans as if they were a toilet. It was acceptable to throw trash out of your car window and keep driving, no matter how many Native Americans they made cry. They were disgusting.

In my home state of New Jersey, their idea of recycling was to light it on fire. Everything from leaves and boxes to newspapers and plastic bottles was burned right in your yard. Their small brains thought this was a good idea because if you light it on fire, it disappears. And so does your house. And your neighbor's house. And any kid in town who has asthma.

There were no good old days. It's a fantasy. Everyone figures it must have been better before. It wasn't. Every one of those beautiful Norman Rockwell paintings is a lie. Lawrence Welk, a lie. Disney Main Street, a lie. It's called Fantasyland for a reason.

So stop complaining from the comfort of your airbag-protected vehicle, press the automatic garage door opener, go inside, pop some Advil, and watch TV in your soft cotton underwear.

MASSAGES ARE FOR SISSIES

When my friend and fellow comedian Kira Soltanovich invited me to join her at a Russian bathhouse, she left out the part about when a man beats you repeatedly in your privates with a bundle of oak branches. This is why I don't trust spas. I sign up because I'm exhausted and end up leaving more confused and tormented than when I went in.

These partially naked misunderstandings happen all the time. I'm not an expert on these spa treatments, but I do know that if you're getting your eyebrows waxed, they shouldn't ask you to take your pants off. This happened to my wife when we were on vacation and she's still trying to figure out what happened.

But every once in a while I find myself standing in a terry-cloth robe and little white slippers with a glass of lemon water in my hand. It's tough to feel manly in this situation. I always picture my grandfather, flanked by other men who fought in World War II, as he glares at me: "And just who the hell do you think you are?"

I rationalize that it's precisely my freedom to get a massage that they fought for. I know that's not likely what they were thinking but sometimes I have a real kink in my neck and there's only one way to get it out.

When I met up with Kira I had been traveling too much, sleeping in way too many bad hotel rooms and cramped airline seats, and I was starting to curl up like a Japanese beetle. This can make you feel a lot older than you are, and if you don't get straightened out once in while, you end up like those old people who are permanently in the shape of the letter "C."

Kira was excited by my pathetic condition.

"We'll go to *banya* for *venik*!" she said. (*Venik* is pronounced "veni-key.")

Kira was born in the Soviet Union and while she is very American she has a genetic obsession with *banya*, which is a Russian bathhouse. Like the rest of her people, she "enjoys the sweating very much." She also has the Russian trait of being very secretive, and when I asked her for details about where we were going, she changed the subject and told me I would find out soon.

"It sounds fun," I said.

"Oh, it's not," she said with a devious smile.

When we checked in it seemed to have the same soothing spa vibe of the places I'd visited before. There was a nice eucalyptus smell, some soothing new age music, and a beautiful, spiritually centered woman at the desk. Kira told her that we were there for *venik* and we were handed locker keys, robes, flip-flops, and a thick, cone-shaped felt hat.

The woman gave us a form to fill out that absolved them of any wrongdoing if we died during *venik*. Another form, another reason to go home. But like a fool, I signed it.

She explained that we had the option of keeping our bathing suits on, but she gave us a look that said it wasn't really an option. As we headed off, Kira explained that keeping our suits on was declaring our lack of respect for the people of Russia, the people who worked here, and most of all her.

"Are you serious?" I asked.

"We have no choice, this is *banya*. I told you it wouldn't be fun."

I wasn't anywhere near the steam room and I was already pouring sweat.

I'm not saying I'm famous, but people do recognize me from time to time, and this was one of those times. Of course, the guy in the locker room didn't acknowledge that he knew me until I was hopping around naked trying to slip into my flip-flops.

"Hey, Tom Papa. You're really funny."

My robe got tangled on the locker. "Hey, thanks, man."

"Have you ever done *venik*?"

"No, first time."

He laughed, shook his head, and walked off. "Good luck."

I closed my robe, put on my weird hat, and shuffled out to the common area. This suddenly felt very Russian. All the softness and soothing tones of the check-in area were gone. Now I stood in a cavernous room covered in wet tile and concrete. Russian accents bounced off the walls as naked people waddled around in nothing but their *banya* hats.

These hats looked like caps that gnomes would wear when they were hanging around the house. They are designed to keep the heat from escaping out of the top of your head and also give you something to focus on when you're trying not to look at a giant Russian man's penis.

Everything was wet. The floors, the walls, the showers that opened up into the room, and the people. They were dripping wet from the Jacuzzis, the showers, and, of course, the sweat. I wasn't sure what I was supposed to do.

"Robe over there," said a small Russian lady while pointing to a series of hooks on the wall.

It's only when you're naked that you suddenly become very aware that you have no place to put your hands. Dangling at my sides is nearly impossible. Putting them on my waist made it look like I was a superhero who's a little too proud of his superfriend. What I really wanted to do was cover up, but no one else was doing that. Quite the opposite. They were all walking around like they did this every day, which they probably did.

"Look at you!" Kira said as she came out of the locker room in her bathing suit. "You really went for it!"

"You said we had to be naked."

"I was joking. But good for you."

You have to understand, Kira and I are pretty much coworkers. This is definitely a #MeToo moment, but who was being violated is anybody's guess.

"Let's *venik!*" she said as she slapped me on my *zhopa*.

First we went in a steam room. That was a good start, because it was so filled with steam that we couldn't see each other. She kept asking if I was nervous for *venik*. I still wasn't clear on what it was, so yes, I was very nervous.

"Don't worry, I'll be there."

I wasn't sure if this was good or bad.

Next, we went to a small swimming pool. This was uncomfortable, because we were no longer alone, we were no longer shrouded in steam, and I was naked. There were other men and women who had no clothes on, but they were much more comfortable with the whole thing than I was.

My strategy was to move quickly. Towel off, dip in the pool, and stay underwater up to my eyes like an alligator. When women came in naked, I focused on staring straight ahead. I used the same strategy as when I go to a yoga class. I feel like it's a female-dominated environment and I'm a visitor who should remain invisible.

Not every guy sees it that way, and certainly not the very tall man who stood with extreme confidence at the edge of our pool. Why was he just standing there completely naked with his hands on his hips? Because apparently he felt that this was his chance to show everyone the burden that God had put upon him. This was his one moment to gain sympathy by showing the world that he had to carry this gigantic appendage around with him every day.

I tried to look away, but it was like trying not to look at a *T. rex* who just walked into the room. I did my best to stare at the ladder, the lounge chair, anything but him.

Kira didn't even try to look away.

Thankfully the Russian woman came in and yelled that it was time for *venik*. As I clambered out of the pool, stumbling on the stairs like a man trying not to have his penis compared to this mythological creature, he asked, "Is this your first time for *venik*?"

"Yes," I said. Everybody laughed.

I wrapped a towel around myself as Kira led me into a two-level sauna. Now as we all know, a sauna is hot. We also know that heat rises. The only reason to build a sauna with two levels is if you are Russian and want to test how strong you are at every turn. Kira smiled.

We climbed the wet, hot tile steps and sat on the wooden bench. Across the room two large sweaty men were sitting in the corner. They looked like they had been there their entire lives. How anyone could stay in there for longer than ten minutes seemed impossible.

Kira asked, "Are you nervous?"

"No. Should I be?"

"Probably."

"I am really hot."

"Just wait."

Suddenly one of the men stood up and said something in Russian and pointed at another wooden bench.

"That's you. Go," Kira said.

I stood up as he said something else in Russian. "He said to leave your towel."

Not totally trusting her translation, I dropped my towel and walked naked over to the bench and sat down. The other man picked up a bundle of sticks that looked pretty much like an entire bush and started walking toward me.

I was no longer concerned that I was naked. I was so hot that I was willing to do whatever I had to do to get this over with. I thought that I might pass out or have a heart attack or even die, but I truly didn't care anymore.

He motioned at the bench with the branches.

"He wants you to lie down," Kira said with a laugh.

As soon as I lay down on my stomach, this man, this large sweaty man who apparently lives in a sauna, started hitting me with the sticks. It wasn't like he was whipping me as much as beating me. Then he dipped them in water and started beating me again, generating extreme heat. This wasn't a massage. This wasn't intended to feel good. What it did was generate extreme heat. More heat than I had felt up to this point. Not just in this sauna but at any point in my entire life.

I felt like I had been coated in hot sauce, rolled in pepper flakes, and stuck in a rotisserie oven.

"*Venik!*" Kira yelled.

"Venik!" the men responded.

And then he stopped. The hot sauna air felt like relief in comparison. I had done it. It was over. My heart was still beating. The Russian man yelled something. I figured it was a congratulatory salute. I said, "Thank you," and got up to leave.

"He said roll over," Kira translated.

I didn't have time to respond. The other man grabbed me and flipped me like a burger patty, and before I could say anything I was beaten with the sticks on my entire front. *Entire* front.

I was about to black out. That same intense heat was now on the tender part of me that I had spent a lifetime protecting. My face had been in trouble before, my chest often neglected, but never this part of me. For forty-odd years I have been this area's Secret Service bodyguard. In a lifetime of organized sports, drunken mishaps, and dance floors, there have been maybe only two times when they've been exposed, let alone injured.

And now, willingly, albeit deliriously, I was exposing them to the aggressive swatting of jungle twigs.

A couple more swats and it was over. I was shocked and stunned. I was confused and vulnerable. Now he did say something triumphant, but I was too weak to rise.

Kira helped me up and led me down the stairs like a doddering old man being helped out of church. We left the sauna and the cool air hit me but had little effect. I was on fire. I thought we were headed back to the locker room, but suddenly I was going up another set of stairs. Why? What was this?

"Plunge pool!"

A forty-degree pool of water. I had no choice. I let her push me into the pot like a resigned lobster. It felt amazing. I came up, smiled, and went back down. Kira cheered.

"I told you this wouldn't be fun."

"No, it's really not," I said.

But somehow I felt great. And strong. And, dare I say, very Russian.

We all need to be unwound once in a while. The stress of our lives physically manifests itself in crooked necks, sore muscles, and furrowed brows, and all the deep-breathing exercises and stretches will do only so much. Sometimes you need something more, something proven throughout history. Something like *venik*.

But I recommend that you keep your shorts on.

HAVE YOU EVER DONE A DNA TEST ON YOUR DOG AND FOUND OUT SHE WAS HALF BOSTON TERRIER AND HALF CAT? I HAVE . . .

PRIMO DNA

My parents and sisters did the whole 23andMe DNA test and it came back with some inconsistent if not surprising results. We always thought that we were mainly Italian with a little German thrown in, but suddenly there was some French and Arabic involved and it threw the whole family tree into an identity crisis.

While I have always been reluctant to send my DNA to some strange lab for fear of cloning or being harvested for organs, my family felt that my test would be key to finding out the real story of our heritage.

So, after spitting in a tube and sending it off to the lab, we finally got an email with the missing information about our family tree. To say we were surprised would be an understatement.

It turns out that there's a good chance I am the next Dalai Lama.

I know. Weird. That's like not even close to Italian.

Now the nagging feeling that I should learn to speak Italian has been replaced with a more nagging feeling that I have to become the spiritual leader of all mankind. I really don't know what to do with this information.

First of all, I'm not a fan of sandals. I don't like them. I prefer a nice shoe or if I'm near a pool maybe some flip-flops. But sandals just don't do it for me. Especially when put together with what appears to be my new outfit—an orange sheet.

Here's something a little embarrassing about my new position: I've never been to Tibet. I'm not even really sure exactly where it is. I know, I know, how can I be the spiritual leader if I can't even find it on a map. I'm not too sure. I'll have to meditate on that one. (That's a Dalai joke.)

I went on the internet to brush up on my Tibetan Buddhism, and I have to say, now that I'm reading up on it all, it does make some sense that I'm the chosen one. For starters, I've always liked incense, and whenever I'm in New York I stop into those Buddhist shops in the Village filled with necklaces and rugs, and most of the time I think about buying some. I never do, but still.

A lot of times the next Dalai Lama is selected when he's a very small child, but in my early years I would have been very tough to find. I was living and going to nursery school in New Jersey. If they had tried looking for me, I doubt they would have had any luck. Back then Jersey didn't take kindly to outsiders, so if they showed up at the mall asking a bunch of questions, there's a good chance they would've gotten punched in the face.

So, now that I know, what do I do? Well, for starters I feel like the monks need to be told, but they're not the easiest to get in touch with either. I've tried Facebook, LinkedIn, Tinder, all the big ones, but no luck. The current Dalai Lama—or, as I now refer to him, the Old Man—has a website but there's no contact info. It's mostly a lot of pictures of him with famous people like Hillary Clinton and Richard Gere.

Now that I'm aware of my destiny, I have to say that it's pretty amazing how much we look alike. Neither of us has a full head of hair, and not only do we both wear glasses, but they seem to be the same exact style. Weird, right? It just happened without either of us planning it, like those twins who are separated at birth and find out when they're reunited that they both love racquetball.

Ever since I found out, I do have an overall sense of calm and I feel like a lot of questions about myself have finally been answered. For instance, I always wondered why I was kind of spiritual when I went away to college. Out of nowhere I started listening to the Grateful Dead and I also had like three dream catchers and a lava lamp in my room. And there was this hippie shop that I would go to in New Hope, Pennsylvania, where I would buy crystals, and I even bought a kaleidoscope once. I didn't even know why, I just did it. Now I know why.

I am a little worried going all in on the whole Dalai Lama thing, because I'm just not sure I'm really ready for this kind of change. I'm extremely busy and I just bought one of those Peloton bikes and it took a long time to set up the Wi-Fi and everything.

And I know, as a Buddhist, you're not supposed to really want material things, but I really love my Tesla, which I'm still trying to pay off. I got it only so I wouldn't have to buy gas, but still the rest of the monks might think it's kind of flashy.

I'm not even sure if the Dalai Lama is allowed to drive. There are no pictures of him driving on the website. What if they can't use electricity? That would be horrible. What if the monks are like the Amish, only with more colorful outfits?

The current Dalai Lama, number fourteen, does go out on tour a lot, so that part of my life wouldn't change too much. And I'm pretty sure that once people find out that I'm the Dalai Lama, it's really going to bump up my numbers on social media. Not that it's the only reason to do it, but being the Dalai Lama is really going to help me define my brand and I'll have like tons of stuff to post on Instagram.

I did check out the Old Man's Twitter account and I'm totally down with the whole "be nice to others" thing that he talks a lot about. I mean, sometimes he can be kind of repetitive, but again, I like how he stays on brand. That's really important.

And it's better than tweeting hateful stuff or responding to all the haters out there. I bet he gets a lot of haters. I'll try not to read the comments if I can help it.

As for my family, they seem to be pretty cool with it. They're taking it much better than when we found out my mother had some French in her. At least this revelation doesn't muddy the family tree with speculation that someone along the line had an illicit affair in a dimly lit bistro. It's much less scandalous that the universe just called upon me.

If only there weren't the sandals.

Maybe I'll be the one to modernize the outfit a little bit, like when nuns decided at a certain point to no longer wear those giant pointy hats. I'm sure that didn't just happen. At some point one of them must have just shown up at breakfast and shocked everyone with a smaller hat. Outrageous as it must have been at the time, it had to be done. I mean, I'm not going to be totally disrespectful. Maybe I'll wear something sandal adjacent, like Crocs or Vans. Does the Dalai Lama ever walk around in the snow? I'm going to have to google that one.

It's pretty remarkable that we're all carrying this ancient DNA around inside of us. Think about it: a part of you has hitchhiked, dated, and survived through the ages. In this vast and violent universe, you are a survivor of the human race and it's up to you to keep it going. And whatever it is that you're made of, I know, without a doubt, that you can do it. And I should know.

I'm the Dalai Lama.

HAVE YOU EVER LOOKED AT
A MENU AND DECIDED THAT
RATHER THAN TRY AND EAT
HEALTHY YOU'RE BETTER
OFF JUST UNDOING THE TOP
BUTTON ON YOUR PANTS?
I HAVE . . . .

I LOVE YOUR LOVE HANDLES

There are a lot of things I like about you.

First off, I love your love handles. There's nothing wrong with love handles. You have them, you're always going to have them, get used to them. I have them, too. When I run down the beach, it looks like two basset hound cheeks are flapping off my sides.

I didn't really like them until I realized what they say about me. Each handle tells a story, like the rings on a tree. They speak of years of good times, ice-cream shops, and hot pastrami sandwiches. They tell people that I've enjoyed my life and there's a good chance that the handles and I are up for anything. We love parties, late-night drinking, and birthday cakes. We eat pies, bake cookies, and aren't afraid of dipping garlic bread into a pot of sauce when no one is looking.

That's why I like yours, too. I know straightaway that we could be friends. When I see someone with six-pack abs, I know we won't have fun because that person doesn't know what fun is. Their idea of a good time is putting on tight shorts and working on their stomach muscles. Someone with love handles is putting on oven mitts and working on baking the perfect cinnamon buns. They're fun.

I also noticed that some of you are big in the caboose. Good for you. A small backside is okay, but it takes real time and care to grow a big one. That really shows character. Nice work. A big rump is even better when it comes with big thighs and little tiny feet. That's the balance that a good life requires.

Much of our appearance is out of our control. I'll admit, when I see a tall, skinny guy in a perfectly tailored suit, I wonder how nice it must feel to naturally look like a fashion model. But I'll never know because I wasn't born that way. When I put a suit on my broad upper body I look like a former wrestler whose wife told him to get a job selling used cars on Route 17.

But at a certain point you have to realize that we're all fat. All of us. You're either really fat, kind of fat, or trying not to be fat. Either way, fat's coming. And that's all right. Do you know why we're fat? Because we're winners. We're one of the first generations that doesn't have to fight for survival. There's always food within arm's reach, it's the perfect temperature everywhere we go. Every day you wake up in America it's a perfect seventy-two and snacky.

So, yeah, we're going to be a little chubby, so don't hate on it. This is it, my friends. You're a grown-up now. This is what you ended up looking like. Game over. So you don't have the body of an Olympic athlete. Well, you're not an Olympic athlete. You're Don, from sales. You have a fat ass, you wear khakis and hike them up when you walk. That's okay, we still like you.

So don't tell me what you're quitting. I don't care. I don't care what your low self-esteem told you that you should quit this week. Every day someone comes up and tells me that they're quitting meat, or gluten, or chewing. I really don't care. You might be feeling bad about yourself, but you're my friend and no diet is going to change that.

Honestly, you looked awful yesterday, you're going to look a little worse tomorrow. Why are we even talking about this? Let's get some ice cream and enjoy the day.

Now look, if you want to feel healthy and exercise helps your mind, I'm all for it. A good run around the block can completely change my mood. But don't starve yourself and run around like crazy just to change your appearance. You're fine just the way you are. Stop pressuring yourself. No one is asking us to take our shirts off for a magazine cover. Unless they start printing *Kind of Chunky Weekly,* we're safe.

You do your best, you try and work out, but you're going to skip. A lot. And that's okay. Don't beat yourself up about it. Do you know why you miss workouts? Because you're an intelligent human being and you know your life isn't being threatened, so you're not going to run your ass off for an hour and a half on some pretend getaway machine.

You're doing great.

My workout now is my Apple Watch. It buzzes once an hour and tells me it's time to stand. And I do. And I feel great about it. It must be why people love the Fitbit. That makes perfect sense to me—strap something to your wrist and count what you normally do as exercise? Get it.

"I walked from my car to my cubicle. Eighty steps!"

"Good job, Carol. You're an athlete now. You should run the 5K. Just a couple more steps, you can do it."

Look, I don't want to be irresponsible. Don't die. You seem nice, so just don't die. That's all you've got to do. That should be the only thing on the Post-it note on your refrigerator: "Don't

Die." And act accordingly. Walk the dog the long way. Touch your toes once in a while.

Don't die.

You don't want to wake up in the middle of the night sweating for no reason, trying to figure out which is the bad arm to be tingly.

"Do we have any baby aspirin? I think we're supposed to eat baby aspirin, or baby food, or lick a baby? Call the neighbors, see if they'll bring us their baby."

I understand that it's hard to feel good about you, and I'm not going to pretend that I'm always okay with who I am. I'm not. There are times when I hate how I look more than anyone else. I have so many chins and such weird body hair that it wouldn't surprise me to find out that my great-grandfather was an orangutan. But that's only my mind that thinks that way. No one else is thinking that because they don't care. They're too busy worrying about their own chins.

Our minds are our worst critics. We do it to ourselves. That's why I can be completely honest when I say, I love your body. I don't care if it's small and bony or round and plump. You can wear size 56 jeans and have boobs that go in two different directions. I don't care that you wear sweatpants because they're the only things that fit. I don't mind that you're shaped like a watermelon with shoes on. I love all of you. Every blubbery inch of you.

Because you're not me. And when I look at you, I have nothing to worry about.

IT'S DATE NIGHT

I know it sounds corny and it is. I know it sounds like the most unspontaneous thing you could do. And you're not wrong. But it's date night and if you're in a relationship, you really have to do it.

If you don't plan a date, it won't happen, and it has to happen because without it you will never see each other. Sure, you'll see your spouse in the kitchen as they stumble around or run into them when you're brushing your teeth. You'll see them when they're struggling to put on their socks or running down the hallway in search of a new roll of toilet paper, but that's not really *seeing* the person you fell in love with.

And without date night you won't really talk either. Most of your conversations when you are married are about logistics. Who's picking up the kids? What do you have today? Did you drop off the dry cleaning? Not exactly romantic phrases. I'm sure there has never been a romantic novel that ever began with the phrase "The toilet's leaking again."

This is why you need date night.

When you go on a date, you return back to the time when you

were in pursuit of each other. When you were working hard to get them to like you. That's what dating is all about. The problem with marriage is that we already have them and think that because we sealed the deal years ago we no longer have to work at making this person like us. But the truth is, you have to try harder than ever before.

It's much easier to make someone like you when they don't know anything about you. The beginning of a relationship is like a magic trick: a series of distractions and illusions meant to dazzle the audience while not allowing them to focus on the ugly parts of you.

But when you're married they know every single thing that's wrong with you. They've seen all your tricks. They know the real you—what you lie about, what bad habits you have, how you really act when you're under pressure. They know everything. So now more than ever you should buy her a nice gift, get dressed up, and take her somewhere special.

I know it sounds lame. I resisted at first because I considered just the need for date night to be an indication that something must be wrong. That if we were really in love, we wouldn't have to plan for a time to be nice to each other. We should still be as spontaneous as when we first met. Sure, and I still fit in the jeans I wore in high school, I can still drink without getting hung over, and I have enough free time to play video games all day and night.

Life changes, and the truth is that if you care about certain aspects of your life, they need a little more focus.

I'm not saying date night is easy. You don't just show up at dinner and instantly turn into that carefree couple you once were. Of course we're going to talk about what's happening at home, it's unavoidable. That would be like Bill Gates and Mark

Zuckerberg getting together and never mentioning computing. But they don't sleep with each other. We do. So at a certain point we have to stop talking about our business of raising children, caring for pets, fixing the leaky roof and just have a good time.

That's the key. Dates are supposed to be fun. You would never go on a date and spend the entire night talking about the most annoying people you know and all the horrible things they are doing to you. You can vent a little, but at some point you have to turn the conversation back to more romantic pursuits.

I know a couple who never went on date night. They just chugged along for years focused solely on raising their kids. They stuck together, not as a romantic couple but as business partners. And it seemed to really work until the kids went away to school and they were left alone for the first time. They were forced to see each other as a couple once again. They were reeling. They didn't know what to do. It was so bad that before they would go to dinner my friend started making a list of things to talk about. A conversation cheat sheet for the woman he'd been married to for twenty years! So sad and yet so avoidable. If only they had gone on a date or two along the way.

We recently went to a tiki bar. This was perfect. First of all, a tiki bar is unlike any other bar you can enter. It's hard to take anything too seriously when you are surrounded by pictures of hula girls, life-size tiki statues, and blowfish hanging from the ceiling.

This place claimed to be the oldest tiki bar in L.A., with a menu filled with "classic tiki" recipes. Be warned: *Do not drive* to a tiki bar. These fun drinks with their joyful colors and fun names like Zombies and Blue Hawaiian are going to knock you on your butt. Perfect for date night, horrible for driving home.

If you want to quickly stop talking about your kids, or forget you even have kids, order a couple of Scorpions and put some fun music on the jukebox. Within minutes we were laughing and dancing together. Just the two of us as we always were.

You know date night is working if you're flirting again. Flirting with this person you fell so deeply in love with that you promised to stay with them to the end of your days is a sign that you've found your way back.

The next morning was painful, and I felt like maybe the end of our days was upon us. I found multiple paper umbrellas on my pillow and my kids gave me a look at breakfast that told me we'd come home way too drunk and loud.

But we were happy.

As Cynthia and I buzzed through the kitchen, we didn't have time to talk about the night before and all our tiki fun because we were right back to work. That conversation will have to wait until next week when date night rolls around again.

HAVE YOU EVER GOTTEN UP SO EARLY FOR A FLIGHT THAT WHILE YOU WERE BOARDING YOU REALIZED YOUR UNDERWEAR WAS ON THE OUTSIDE OF YOUR PANTS? I HAVE . . .

I'M GOING TO MARS!
IF MY WIFE WILL LET ME

I'm going to Mars. It's all planned out. I've watched some reports, checked out some websites. It looks pretty amazing. All I have to do now is convince my wife to let me go.

Elon Musk says I have to go, or that "we humans" have to go. I haven't spoken to him directly, he seems like he might be tough to talk to, but he's right that the mission is necessary to preserve humankind. There's only one hitch—we can't come back. It's a one-way ticket to a rough and inhospitable planet, kind of like a one-way ticket to Staten Island.

I'll admit that I'm a little worried that I'll get there and find out that it's not as good as the brochure and then have to stay there for the rest of my life. This happened to me once on a road trip to Lancaster, Pennsylvania. They made it look like a quaint hotel hosted by a nice Amish family, but it turned out to be a creepy hotel hosted by a man who looked like he just got out of prison on a technicality. In that case I just got in the car and was back home in three hours.

I can't do that on this trip, but ultimately I'm okay with that. It's a risk I'm willing to take, and unlike being in Lancaster, however poor the accommodations, I imagine it will be offset by the fact that I'm standing on Mars. That's pretty cool stuff. If only my wife thought the same way.

I don't know what her deal is. She seems to think that I'm going on a golf weekend with my friends till the end of time, but I don't think they'll even have golf there. Now that I think of it, they actually did golf on the moon. That must have really irked the wives down on Earth trying to look supportive in front of the reporters for *Life* magazine.

But seriously, how can I deny all of civilization? They're counting on me. How can I sit down here wasting time at Taco Bell and rubbing sunscreen on my belly by the pool when there are planets to populate? What if it's my destiny? My manifest destiny?

This must be why Lewis and Clark weren't married. They couldn't focus on their journey out west while someone was following them around asking how long they'd be gone.

Could you imagine Clark putting on his coonskin jacket, saying, "No, I told you I'm leaving *this* Saturday."

"Well, change it."

"I can't change it, Lewis is waiting down by the canoe. You'll just have to go to the Bernsteins' bar mitzvah without me."

"Why?"

"Why? Because I have to cross the Mississippi and cause problems for the indigenous people, that's why."

This is what I'm dealing with as I prepare for my trip to the giant red planet. I'm thinking about what to pack and my wife is acting like it's not even happening.

I'm assuming there won't be any training. I hope there's not.

That's not going to work for me. I mean, I'll go to Mars but I don't want to have to join a gym to do it. It's not like I'm going to have to steer the ship or anything. I see my role more as a special guest: the funny guy who makes an appearance now and again. When things get boring and people are a little homesick, I come into the cafeteria, crack some jokes, do something funny with a carrot, that kind of thing. Like one of the guest actors on *The Love Boat*.

And that reminds me: As a special guest, I am not flying coach. That won't happen. I don't fly coach to Baltimore, I'm definitely not flying coach all the way to Mars. I hope Elon understands that. I wonder if they'll have those sleep pod things like they do on Big Planes. Those are really cool and come with a bunch of movies and a kit with a sleep mask, earplugs, and a pair of socks. The socks are always a little weird to me, but I guess with so many people out there who think that flip-flops are acceptable travel footwear, regardless of their age or how disgusting their feet are, maybe the socks are a good idea.

The best pods I ever experienced were on a flight from JFK to Dubai on Emirates airline. It was the best flight of my life. I got lucky and some company paid for the whole thing. I was waiting in the lounge with my first-class ticket on a late-spring night, staring out at the giant plane that I was going to be boarding. It was one of those behemoths with two stories. It made more sense to try and fly an apartment building.

I was trying to act like this was nothing new to me. That waiting in the first-class international lounge for my flight to the Middle East was just something that I did all the time. It's hard not to look like a rube in a situation like this, and I was definitely a rube.

I don't know if you're aware of this, but everything is free in the international lounge, which is disconcerting when you're used to having to pay for everything that you can barely afford your whole life. It's not until you hang around the rich that you realize how much free stuff they get.

There was a full bar with bottles of expensive liquor just sitting out for the taking without a bartender, hostess, or police officer anywhere in sight. There were giant buffets of food that looked like a spread for some oil tycoon or a drunk Warren Buffett. I wonder if Warren Buffett is aware that his name is one letter away from being Warren Buffet. Someone should tell him, it could give him some good material when he's at brunch.

I felt like I was stealing and didn't want to get caught. I'd sneak up to the bar, take something, and scurry back to my seat like a squirrel who sees a pile of nuts and doesn't trust that it's not a trap. I nabbed a beer and ran back to my seat. When no one came to arrest me, and I felt safe again, I bolted back up, grabbed some sushi, put a few in my cheeks, and ran off like a child who comes across candy he's not supposed to have.

This lounge was so fancy that when it was time to board my flight, a woman came and whispered in my ear and walked me to the gate. I did my best not to spit out the giant wad of cashews in my mouth.

When I boarded the plane they led me up a spiral staircase to the second level. Stairs on a plane are not normal. A lot of people don't have stairs in their home. I was expecting a nice seat, but what I discovered was pretty much my own room. It was gigantic. I poked my head up from my pod like a gopher and looked around, but I was completely alone. It was just me and seven of the most beautiful female flight attendants I had ever seen, and their entire job on this flight would be to do nothing but wait on me.

They brought out steaks, salads, asparagus in hollandaise

sauce, ice cream sundaes, exotic chocolates, entire bottles of Bordeaux, and a coffee service that seemed to combine all the knowledge of all the coffee that had ever been made. All I had to do was sit in my nest with my mouth open like a baby bird.

I didn't want to sleep and miss any of it, but I was only able to hang for so long. I fell into a long, deep sleep as the plane flew over the top of the planet, straight above the North Pole. I dreamed vividly about the Middle East, a place that I knew very little about. This was a part of the world that I had constructed in my mind from slanted news stories and public school geography classes that taught us to be afraid.

I remember waking up, not understanding how long I had slept or how many time zones I had crossed. I stood up and stretched. There's something about waking up in a place that gives you more ownership of it. This plane was now my domain, and as I made my way to the back I discovered a full round bar. I startled the staff, as if the captain had just made an appearance on deck unannounced. I gave them a little smile to put them at ease and, again trying to act like I did this all the time, ordered a gin fizz.

I've never had a gin fizz in my life. I don't even like gin all that much and have no idea where the fizz comes from. I wanted to sound like James Bond but ended up sounding like James Bond's silly gay cousin. But after two or three drinks and some free bar snacks, I regained my mojo and chatted them up and got some good solid laughs. Just like *The Love Boat*.

I ate some more, drank some more in my pod, and watched a bunch of movies as the flight attendants came by every three minutes or so just to deliver another smile. It was a twelve-hour flight and one of the nicest times I could remember on sea, land, or sky. I didn't want it to end.

The rest of the trip I was in Dubai and Beirut, and as you can probably predict, I met beautiful people and learned that they were just like you and me.

As great as the Middle East was, I did start to miss home after a while. I was with people, but not my people. I don't mean my countrymen, I mean my loved ones. My wife. My family. My dog. My car. My TV.

That's always the way. It's always fun to travel, but if you don't have your family with you at a certain point, what are you doing? At a certain point you're no longer traveling, you're running away from home.

I guess this is what my wife is thinking. I mean, I don't want to leave them forever. A one-way ticket to Mars is like announcing to your family the exact day that you're going to die. While it's somewhat convenient and allows you to get all your paperwork in order, it's probably better for them to be surprised. It's better to get a call from the hospital than know he's out there playing gin rummy on some other planet.

But I have faith. I have faith Elon will figure out a way to make it a round-trip ticket. Lewis and Clark eventually went back home and got married and had nice, normal lives. And that's what I'm going to do. I'll go, hang out for a couple of years, boost up my social media, and eventually return safely home.

As a gesture, for my willingness to cut my trip short, I would like to request that my wife and kids throw a nice ticker-tape parade or at the very least have a WELCOME HOME banner over the fireplace and a big bowl of Butterfingers.

There's no way she can say no to that. Right?

HAVE YOU EVER FALLEN ASLEEP DURING THE NEWS AND WOKEN UP TO A HORROR MOVIE AND YOU COULDN'T TELL THE DIFFERENCE? I HAVE . . .

PLAY BY THE RULES

As much as I root for us all, there are some people out there who are not playing by the rules. And rather than give them a free pass I think it's important, for the good of all humanity, that we call them out.

I don't like sneaky people.

They're wormy. I don't like worms. They're always trying to get one up on the next guy but don't have the courage to fight for it, so they just wiggle and slither around. I see them at the airports all the time. In the last couple of years I've been on planes pretty much every week. And I've seen a lot of sneaks.

They're like scavengers on the African plains, skulking around with hunched, guilty shoulders and shame-filled eyes. They slither around like hyenas, avoiding eye contact because they live in a constant state of being found out for their miserly deeds and petty thefts. And make no mistake, they are stealing from us. They think we are suckers and that's what bothers me most of all.

In the airports they cut in line. No one liked a cutter when we were little and no one likes one now. It's one of the first social violations we learn to detect, and whoever cut got hit with a lunch box. The problem with stopping these people as adults is that we no longer have lunch boxes and most of us don't want to fight with a stranger.

But at a certain point something has to be done. I confronted some of these creeps not too long ago. I was standing in line patiently waiting to board a plane, and admittedly I was a little cranky and tiring of my fellow man. I was lined up with the rest of zone one when this guy in his sixties and his wife started worming their way past everybody. We had all been there for a while. We had established a quick social order and were getting along just fine. And here they come, acting like they didn't see us, slithering their way in and cutting us all.

You don't fly for a month straight witnessing injustice without eventually reaching the breaking point. You get to the point where, in the name of justice, you find yourself having to stand up for yourself and the rest of the class.

"Excuse me," I said. This was a great start. Here is the voice of someone who might have been wronged but is about to politely ask a question on behalf of everybody else.

"Did you not notice all of us who are standing here in line?" This is another great phrasing, because it gives the worm an opportunity to repent. I also pointed out "all of us," letting them know that we're a group, that while they were probably shoplifting gum from the Hudson News, we came together and have established laws and you're breaking them and there will be punishment if you make the wrong choice.

The husband played dumb, looking at his crumpled-up boarding pass as if he were seeing it for the first time. This is a classic technique. His wife took a more arrogant approach and snapped back.

"Don't worry, we're not taking your place," she said.

"This isn't about me. This is about all of us. We are all in line and there's absolutely no reason you can come up with that will justify you cutting in front of all of us, as if we aren't here," I said.

This wasn't exactly elegant, but it's sometimes difficult to speak when you want to scream. I did manage to throw in "cutting," which got everyone's attention.

"Cutting? Who's the cutter? Where are they? Who has a lunch box?"

The gate attendant made an announcement that boarding was about to begin. They wouldn't move. The husband kept up his dementia act while his wife glared at me and they both inched ahead, as if it were out of their control, that momentum was simply pulling them along.

I was angry. My usually exemplary, passive-aggressive witticisms were thrown to the wind. I was in shock. I was at a loss. Who does this? What kind of people act this way?

"Shit People."

That's who. And that's what I declared them to be. Out loud. In a crowd.

Although I tend not swear, it was accurate; that's exactly what they were. But once you use profanity you lose supporters. Maybe the people in zone six would cheer, but with all the older, conservative people in zone one, you lose fans pretty quickly.

I tried making eye contact with one of my line mates but they weren't having it. I was on my own, but I was determined, so I said it again.

Now, the good thing about profanity is that it signals to everyone that you are willing to break the social norms and you have become a bit of a wild card. Everyone wants to know how far you're willing to go. What will you say next? Will you turn violent? Everyone was on edge, except the two of them. They just kept moving forward. The wife gave me a nasty smile like she'd heard it all before and there was nothing I could do to stop her.

I was stuck. As much as I wanted to give them both a spinning karate kick, I could do only so much. They were winning.

Until they ran into the sheriff.

The sweet and mighty gate attendant. She was our last hope, but you never know how this will go. Will she let them go through because she's working at this too long and just can't be bothered? Will she not notice them until they're halfway down the ramp? Or will she lay down the law?

The sneaks handed over their boarding passes, while making some lame joke to win her over, another wormy technique.

"Hold on," she said. "This is zone five."

The husband pretended not to hear.

The arrogant wife spoke up. "Oh, we're pre-boarding."

"No, you're not," said the gate attendant.

I was as excited as a child on Christmas morning. I was giddy. I was restored.

"Yes, we are. We did it on the flight out," lied the wife out of her lying lips on her lying face.

"If you were pre-board, it would say on your boarding pass. It does not. It says zone five."

With nothing left to say, the husband decided to make a run for it but was way too slow.

"Sir, get out of line and wait your turn like everybody else." She held out her arms to block them. "Now!"

Oh, was I happy. We all were. Someone clapped. A stranger patted me on the back.

The worms put their heads down in shame and walked off to the principal's office. I made eye contact with the wife. I didn't have to say it. We both knew.

Everybody knew.

I moved forward with my boarding pass with the joy and confidence that comes with knowing that you did the right thing. I handed it to the gate attendant, excited to be so close to someone so strong.

I gave her a reassuring look and said, "Great job."

"Ooh, that makes me so mad. If there's one thing I can't stand in this world, it's sneaks and liars."

I nodded in agreement and said, "Shit People."

She laughed. "You got that right, honey."

Will those people do it again? Probably. Some people are just horrible. While the rest of us are trying to get along, looking out for each other, they're interested only in themselves. I don't like them and I definitely don't respect them.

And every once in a while the good guys win.

HAVE YOU EVER BEEN OUT
TO DINNER WITH PEOPLE
WHO TOLD THE WAITER TO
NOT BRING BREAD TO THE
TABLE AND YOU ASKED TO
MOVE TO ANOTHER TABLE?
I HAVE....

I'M SO BAKED

How do you find meaning in your life when you know that you are just one tiny speck tooling around in a giant universe? What are the answers? How do you live with purpose? I don't really know, but I sure have been spending a good amount of my time baking bread and that seems to do the trick.

I bake a lot of bread. I make it, bake it, and eat it. I think about it when I'm awake and dream about it when I'm asleep. I look for new recipes on my favorite bread sites. I have a tower of books on nothing but bread. My Instagram is filled with bakeries from around the world. I visit those bakeries when I'm traveling and spy on their ovens and their flour and their techniques.

I love the smell of it. I love the taste of it. I love what I can do with it. I love sharing it. I give it to friends and family. I send it to strangers in brown paper bags that I bought just for the bread.

To my wife's dismay and against her wishes, I have taken over a large portion of the kitchen with breadbaskets, mixers, and flour containers. I get upset if my kids forget to put a fork in the dishwasher, but I have no problem with the mountains of flour piled on the floor.

I order my flour from a company in Utah called Central Milling. It costs more to ship it than it does to buy it. It comes in fifty-pound bags. I always know when it arrives because it lands on the front steps with a thud like an elephant taking a seat.

I have to drag it into the house like a dead body. Not that I have ever carted around a dead body, but I can only imagine it wouldn't be easy. I feel good when I open the box and see the giant bag. It means something. It means that I bake. That I take it seriously. And that my wife thinks I'm annoying.

The other side of the kitchen is the bread box, a giant cutting board that is just for bread, and bread knives. A good serrated bread knife is a must. The sensual difference of a smooth slicing of a loaf of bread is palpable.

Baking bread the way I do is not easy. It's a three-day process from the time I decide to make it to the moment I am stuffing a slice in my mouth. It can be complicated, there's a lot that can go wrong, and I love every minute of it.

It begins by taking the sourdough starter out of the refrigerator and feeding it flour and water. Yes, feed it.

The sourdough starter is a living organism. It's living yeast like the plant in *Little Shop of Horrors* that needs to be fed. You can create one of these pets by mixing up a bowl of flour and water and leaving it on the counter. Microscopic natural yeast that is flying all around us will enter the mixture and eat it. This becomes a mini ecosystem of yeast feeding and extracting gas. It's believed that someone, probably in ancient Egypt, accidentally stumbled upon this process and this supercool baker made the first bread more than four thousand years ago.

I have two of these creatures living in Mason jars inside my refrigerator.

Although people name theirs, I have not. We were, however,

featured on the cover of the *New York Times* food section when the prolific Sam Sifton interviewed my starter and me and sent a photographer to snap some shots of us. This caused confusion in my comedian friends, who thought someone had stolen my identity.

When it's time to bake, they get brought out onto the counter and fed repeatedly for a couple of days, essentially putting the yeast into a feeding frenzy before it can be added to the flour for the creation of the bread dough.

My only regret about this lengthy process is that I don't have more time to do this. My life has been so busy over the last two years that if I can get a week or two at home without leaving, it's a luxury. It's gotten to the point where I gauge my touring schedule by the amount of bread I'm able to bake. If there's bread, I'm home and I'm happy.

My basic bread is a country loaf. A round, rustic-looking bread that is mainly malted wheat flour mixed with all-purpose white flour and a touch of rye. I bake these two at a time in cast-iron Dutch ovens that allow me to generate a lot of heat and steam when the lids are shut.

I also bake bagels, the best in L.A., and an olive loaf that is insanely good. Green and kalamata olives mixed with herbes de Provence and lemon zest. It reaches another level with cream cheese spread on it.

One of my favorite things to do with the bread is make the Gentleman's Breakfast. It's so good it will break your heart. The night before, you mix chopped garlic and diced anchovies into soft butter. The next morning, you pull it out of the refrigerator and spread healthy portions of it on toasted country bread. A fried egg on the side is optional. I'm telling you that a bite into this with some great coffee on the side is transformative, but I don't recommend booking any meetings or romantic interludes that day.

Another favorite that might make your skin crawl but is heaven to me is to spread cream cheese on a thick piece of toast, spread sardines across, and top with capers and olive oil. Gadzooks, it's delicious. It's not as salty as the anchovies, but it has a natural, more fragrant taste and apparently is crazy good for you.

The kids love avocado toast, almond-butter toast, or just plain butter with scrambled eggs.

It's the baking for others that makes the experience really special. With each step of the actual baking process, the oven door is opened and some baking-bread aroma escapes into the house. Everyone is alerted that something is being made for them.

Someone is baking bread that can be enjoyed and made into grilled cheese or a simple toast on the way out the door to school. Someone cares.

So, this is what I do. I fail. I succeed. I have glorious loaves that I'm proud of. I have flat failures that I quickly put in the garbage before anyone can see. But with practice things got easier and I developed an intuition about it all.

I know by the weight of the metal scooper in my hand how much flour will be measured out on the scale. I know the same about how much weight is in a cup of water, how long the dough has to rest. I know before it goes into the oven with very little variance how much it will rise. It is the knowing that has made this practice transformative.

Whatever you do and do well, your swimming, your running, your painting, these are more than hobbies, they're an extension of you. The real you. The simple act of doing something well over time stirs up a part of your subconscious that even you may not be aware of. And make no mistake, that is nothing short of magical.

It's magical because we're dealing with unknowable parts of ourselves. Parts that are difficult to explain. I like that.

I love the writer Gabriel García Márquez, but I find it funny that when critics write about him they feel the need to describe him as writer of mystical realism. I see him simply as a novelist, and anywhere he wants to take me is just fine, and the idea that magic enters his work only tells me that he was open, truly open, to every aspect of the world, both seen and unseen.

Doing something that feels worthwhile and valuable taps into that same space. Of course, he also wrote about ghosts showing up and mingling with the living, but again, who's to say.

I had the opportunity to travel around the United States and meet bakers in different cities. This was for a TV show called *Baked* that took me to some of the highest-acclaimed artisans of baked goods. I was struck by the similarities not only in the people but also in their stories.

Many were baking because it had been a craft in the family that was passed down throughout the years. But many more started off in another career that they thought was the responsible way to make money. But after baking as a hobby, they eventually became so enamored with the process that they all took a leap of faith and turned their passion into their career.

Over and over I heard how they left a job in IT or law or computer engineering and opened a bakery, and even though they may be working even harder, longer hours now, they are much happier. And not click-your-heels, phony Instagram happy but truly content from living a good, purposeful, simple life.

When we're looking for purpose or a reason for being, the answer is really in the doing.

It's not in the picture we post of ourselves on vacation, it's in the sewing and hammering and cutting and sawing. It's in the dancing and dicing and singing and sketching.

Start small. Start by helping someone. Start by loving something. And just start doing it. Whatever it is. Because that will turn into a passion and introduce you to a part of you you'll be happy to know.

But what do I know? I just bake bread.

A COUPLE OF REALLY BAD DAYS

We all run into rough patches. Times when it seems fate just wants to mess around with us like a vindictive cat toying with a newly caught mouse. You can try and escape, you can try and turn things around, but sometimes all you can do is ride it out.

This is one of those times.

It's January and there's a giant blizzard on its way. The weather reports have been grim and constant, sending most people on the East Coast running for cover and fighting their way to their homes to huddle with their loved ones beside the fire.

I am alone on a cold train, hurtling along icy tracks to a casino, deep in the woods of Connecticut.

I try and spend as little time as possible in casinos and now there's a good chance I'm going to be stuck in one, possibly forever. This is a dumb thing to do, but I have a show, and like many cold, soggy performers before me, I have no choice but to get to the gig.

I boarded in Penn Station, which is a bleak New York underground hub that makes the journey less like the start of a trip than it does a prison jailbreak.

They make everybody stand in front of a giant board that lists all the upcoming departures in rotating signage. When your train comes up for boarding, a track number is added and everyone runs off to beat the competition to the escalator that takes you belowground even more, to your dirty train. In most places this may be an organized way to shuttle travelers around; in New York it's the beginning of a riot.

It doesn't take more than a little pressure to watch the worst part of people's nature rise up. What seemed like a rather docile woman carrying a Trader Joe's bag filled with gifts for her grandchildren suddenly becomes a conniving monster, hell-bent on destroying everyone in her way. I was in her way.

This is what happens when they start delaying the departure time. You can feel the mob begin to turn because they've been betrayed. You kept up your part of the bargain—you bought your ticket, you showed up on time—and now it's clear that you've been lied to. Anger starts to mix with nervousness, which adds to stress, which results in sweating. A lot of sweating.

This betrayal is also what has turned flying in this country into a blood sport. By chipping away at the size of the seats and the size of the overhead, by creating a separation of class even within coach, the airlines have pitted the travelers against each other in a battle that resembles a cockfight. It may not be in most people's nature to act this way, but the airlines have a real way of drawing it out.

Once we were all on board the train, this horde of disoriented people with low blood sugar had to scramble and find a seat. Normally you try and pick the best person to sit next to, who is going to be the least offensive, less rude, and who doesn't smell like old tacos. But today, we didn't have the luxury of sizing anyone up; this was all about grabbing whatever seat you could find or risk having to stand in between cars like a hobo on the rails. Being picky about your seat on Amtrak doesn't really make sense anyway. There is literally no difference between a business-class seat on Amtrak and the restroom on Amtrak.

As I settled into my seat, my stomach was making noises. My plan to eat at the end of the trip was thrown out the window thanks to the delay. I needed food and had no choice but to head to the café car. This isn't the luxurious café car you've seen in the movies, unless you've seen a movie about people eating salty snacks with their fingers and warm beer from a can. This is the real-life café car that must have been designed and built by a farmer used to feeding livestock and smelled a lot like the men's room at Yankee Stadium.

I was doing everything I could to get a hot dog and most of a beer in my mouth as I hung on to a railing squeezed between two gorillas in suits at the bar. I got a second beer and loaded up on pretzels and Fritos before taking the wobbly walk back to my seat.

It's amazing what a couple of quick beers can do to the view of any apocalyptic landscape. Suddenly the people around me didn't seem so bad. I was actually feeling pretty good. Alcohol gets the job done yet again, which speaks to the never-ending popularity of airport bars, Irish taverns, and Margaritaville. For all the talk of the dangers of climate change and economic collapse, if you really want to see the world in chaos, close the bars.

However, my good mood was short-lived as I overheard a loud businessman giving the bleak snow forecast and was reminded that I was on a train to a prison filled with slot machines.

If you like to gamble, this probably sounds pretty good. My father loves to gamble, because he's actually won a bunch of times so he knows what that feels like. I have no idea what that experience is like. Not only do I not win but I can change the luck of a table just by looking at it.

When I was a kid we would vacation at the Jersey Shore, about an hour away from Atlantic City. The entire time we were swimming in the ocean and making sandcastles he was plotting his escape, which always involved bringing me along as if it were a father-and-son outing.

I knew what he was up to. He really wanted no part of me and my bad mojo when he was gambling, but he figured he could bring me along, toss me twenty dollars to go play the slots with the other ladies, and he'd be free to gamble the night away.

I kind of enjoyed it. The cocktail waitresses give out free drinks when you gamble, without checking your ID. So I'd play some games, order some gin and tonics, and hang out with the seniors who came down on the bus.

The old people never asked my age, they were just happy to have someone to talk to. They liked to gossip, and after a couple of drinks I was filled with questions and strong opinions.

"What do you mean she didn't give you your dish back? That's just plain rude," I'd say as Delores lit my cigarette. "If you ask me, I'd say she's a little jealous of you."

We'd play the slots until our money ran out, smoke a couple more cigarettes, and have a good old time. I didn't realize it then, but I was definitely being flirted with. There are only so many times an eighty-year-old woman accidentally puts her hand on your lap.

Eventually I'd get tired and want to go home. There was no use asking my father to leave, he would have stayed there the rest of his life if he could. I knew that if I wanted to go, I would have to use my superpower to end whatever lucky streak he had going on.

He was once on a hot streak playing craps, throwing dice to the screaming encouragement of the crowd he was helping to win. I could see he was having a good time and probably winning a good amount of money, but I was tired. So I walked up and stood behind him, and for the first time in an hour he threw craps. The crowd groaned, went silent, and walked away. The fun was over. He didn't even have to turn around; he knew I was there.

"I'll get the car," he mumbled.

I get why people want to go. These casinos are expertly designed with the right amount of flash and noise to keep people amused and entertained. But even for those who enjoy being there, it's a nervous system overload. And when you're there for work, which was why I was headed there, it's as amusing as a colonoscopy.

The train was rocking back and forth from the wind that was just ahead of the coming storm. I looked at the weather app on my phone and the radar showed a monster storm, bigger than five states, that seemed to be moving just as fast as we were.

I was returning to a comedy club up there that I hadn't played in a couple of years, where the crowds are really drunk and obnoxious. You might think that there's no way the crowd could be the same as when I was there two years ago, but you'd be wrong. Certain places bring out a certain something in people.

The casino is about an hour's drive from the train station through normally beautiful countryside. This was the land of the Mohegan tribe who sued the U.S. government to get their land back and by gaining a sovereign reservation were allowed to build a casino and restore their wealth. I'm not sure if this really made everybody "even steven," but it definitely helped. I wonder why we never hear about giving casinos to African Americans throughout the South. It might be something to consider.

We finally pulled into the station and everyone scrambled through the light snow into their families' cars. In the old days, about three years ago, I'd have to take a taxi driven by a man of questionable moral standing who was very likely drunk. Now I order up an Uber, which is pretty much the same guy who drives his own car.

I was nauseated and my head hurt and his car smelled like old shoes. In moments like this I just need to stop moving. Literally. That's the hardest part of being on the road, the constant motion. I sometimes feel like an astronaut in training who never gets past the vomit rocket stage.

For the first time in my career I have uttered the words "I'm away too much." There's a steeliness that one needs in order to not be lonesome on the road. This isn't a disregard for the joy of being home and spending time with your family. But at the same time, if I were to wrap myself around my home life like a giant quilt, I would never leave.

And I have to leave. It's my job to leave. I think.

I was late. I checked into my room, which I have to say was pretty nice. I showered and headed down to the club. My buddy Andy was the opening act, and he was onstage doing his best and that normally is enough to get the crowd going. But not tonight. This crowd was off. My mood started to sour.

Any hope I had of getting through the night unscathed disappeared as soon as I got onstage. Immediately after my introduction, someone in the third row threw up on his table. When someone throws up it's like a bomb going off. In slow motion I could see everyone recoil, fall back on their chairs, and take cover. The drunk guy just looked around like he was just as surprised as anybody else.

The night was horrible. The crowd was so drunk and loud that they started heckling each other. There I was in a suit and tie, thousands of miles from home, performing material I have worked on for the last two years in front of what was essentially a bachelor party. It's difficult in these moments to hate not only the entire audience but all of mankind.

I walked offstage and into the elevator, went back to my room, and peeled off my clothes. What were flurries a mere three hours before was now a blizzard pounding into my windows on the thirty-fifth floor.

The owner of the club had given me Rice Krispies Treats that his wife had made. I was so hungry that I ate two immediately. They must have had something in them because within a half hour I couldn't feel my hands.

I don't remember how I got there, but I suddenly found myself at the slots, drinking a gin and tonic with a group of old ladies, like the good old days. We must have had a good time because when I woke up in the morning there was bright red lipstick on my cheeks.

Fighting a terrible headache, I looked out the window and the entire world was white. The storm was fierce. I checked my phone. The Saturday night shows were canceled, as was my flight the next day, along with all the other flights that were leaving from the Hartford airport.

Just as I had forecasted, I was very stuck. And very alone.

I wandered downstairs to the casino. Even the people who came here on their own looked depressed. The slot machines didn't jingle as much as sigh. I looked around the way someone does after being hit in the head, trying to make sense of the world.

My initial instinct was to eat and drink. Maybe a large fried-egg sandwich and spicy Bloody Mary would change things around or at least bring a little of the humor back to the situation. Most of the restaurants were closed. The blizzard not only had trapped the guests in the hotel but had snowed the workers in their homes.

"Dude! You were hilarious!"

A big lug in an even bigger flannel shirt came running up to me. He was covered in snow and looked like a snowman who just came in from hunting.

"Oh, thanks," I said as I reluctantly shook his hand.

"What are you doing now?"

"I'm not sure." I really wasn't.

His energy was frantic and too determined for this sleepy, snowed-in morning. I was really afraid he was going to ask me to play in the snow with him and slowly started moving away.

"When do you go home?"

"Depends on the storm, I guess, the airport's closed."

"Yeah, but Newark's open."

"That doesn't help me."

"Why, they don't fly to L.A.?" He laughed and punched me in the arm with his snowy fist.

"I mean, I'm not in Newark. I'm stuck in a casino in the ass end of Connecticut."

"Yeah, but dude, I'm going to Jersey and I have a truck."

"Uh . . . what, now?"

"Yeah, man, go get your shit. I mean, if you want to. I'll drive you there."

"Are you sure? Aren't the roads closed?"

"Dude, we don't need roads. We have a truck!"

Yes, we did. We did have a truck. And a man who was a part

of that horrible crowd that was out to kill me ended up being one of the funniest and kindest people I had met all year. We laughed, skidded, and bonded all the way to Jersey, and pretty quickly, too.

Before I knew it, I was headed home in a cramped middle seat, nibbling on Cheez-Itz. Who can complain about that?

BE A GOOD GUY

Be a good guy. At least give it a try.

Don't yell and scream in places where it's not cool to yell and scream.

Don't start fights and don't get in fights for no reason.

If someone is being hurt and they need your help, fight away.

Don't curse in front of children.

Don't put testicles on the back of your pickup truck.

Don't blast your music or your engine. No one is impressed.

Be kind to women.

Don't talk to anyone about what she said.

Don't tell anyone what you did together when you were alone.

Don't act like you're deserving of anything. Earn it.

Go to work.

Be kind.

DO YOU EVER WISH YOU WERE SMARTER? NOT ME!

Being really stupid might be the way to go. To be nice they call it "uninformed" or "distracted from reality," but let's face it, they're not reading this anyway so let's call it like it is. You see them out there. I'm talking about the people who don't watch the news, don't bother with newspapers, and eat candy for dinner. This isn't a knock, I'm actually envious because they just seem so damn happy.

I know it makes for a harder life in a lot of ways. You pay for it at other times, like when you have to use something complicated like a toaster. But sometimes it sure seems nice.

Don't you think that part of our cultural unhappiness might be due to the fact that we just know too much? Small children don't know much about anything and look how happy they are. A kid can happily sit in an empty cardboard box by himself for hours. That's not imaginative, that's just not bright. Sure, he doesn't know how to tie his shoes, but he's not worried about it and he sure as hell isn't bothered about his interest rate. His only interest is sticking stuff in his belly button.

I want to be one of those guys Jimmy Kimmel interviews on the street. You know, the ones who think that Los Angeles is a country or that The Rock is our president. Could you imagine being so carefree that the very question "Who is the president?" is the most shocking thing you've ever heard?

Think about how easy your daily decisions are. Planning dinner is no longer complicated. There's no need for cookbooks and recipes and trips to the store and hours of chopping and dicing. You don't go to the supermarket at all. You go to Taco Bell or McDonald's and the toughest decision you have to make is whether to eat in your car while you're driving.

You know what smart people have? High blood pressure from worrying about all the stuff they know. Then they have to make an appointment with their doctor, and that leads to all sorts of worrying about what insurance they have and how much money they make and how they're going to pay for it. I have a friend that hasn't been to a doctor since the sixth grade. If he finds a mole on his back, he doesn't get it checked out, he names it.

Not me. I know too much. I found a blemish on my leg and spent the next week scaring myself on WebMD. By the end of all my research I was so convinced that I was dying from so many diseases that I started revising my will.

This happens to me all the time. My doctor said I had pre–high blood pressure, so I bought a heart monitor. Horrible idea. Anytime I feel weird or hungry or tired I'm convinced I must be dying. I hook it up to my arm, which immediately makes me more nervous. Then I worry that my wife and kids are going to walk in and catch me checking my blood pressure, which will only cause them to worry. Nothing like seeing your father, the man responsible for paying your bills, sweating in his office attached to some medical equipment. Now it's guaranteed that my numbers won't be good, so I hit the start button over and over again until it finally shows a number that I'm happy with.

And why do I put myself through this? Because I know too much. My friend with the mole doesn't know his blood pressure, he just knows that when he gets chest pains he can make them go away by eating salami and hitting himself in the chest with his fist.

He's much happier than smarter people. I've never met an intellectual doing a cannonball into a swimming pool. He sits at the end of the bar with a glass of Scotch, scowling at everyone because they don't want to discuss philosophy with him.

Why would they? So they can spend all night trying to figure out "Why are we here?" That can never be answered by anyone, which means it was better off that the question was never asked in the first place. You know who doesn't ask that question?

People who can't pronounce the word "philosophy."

Have you ever met a *really* smart person? Someone who can do complicated math in their head and has a vocabulary more extensive than a Scrabble dictionary? They're weirdos. It's like they've been crippled by their intelligence.

Their eyes are small and beady, as if they've seen too much and can't bear to look at anything anymore. Or they have glasses because they've burned their eyes out from all that reading. And they always look nervous. They always look like they know something bad is going to happen. And sure, it's pretty likely that it will happen and that it will be caused by someone dumb, but guess who's not worrying about it at all? The dumb guy.

Smart people buy insurance and fasten their furniture to the walls in case of an earthquake. They wear seat belts and spend their money on emergency kits and stay up late at night making sure they have enough money in the bank. What idiots.

Dumb people are fearless. They have way more fun. When they look at a trampoline they don't see an emergency room, broken bones, and a humiliating YouTube video where everyone will see their dumb accident until the end of time. They look at a trampoline and see a thing to bounce on.

They make ramps that they can jump their bicycle off of. They bungee jump sometimes without a bungee. They have a good time. They see life as a challenge without fear of death because they don't think about death because they don't think. Period.

How great would it be to not know about global warming? You don't think about the planet dying or the rising seas. You don't think about recycling or reusing, all you think about is garbage and not garbage and sometimes you eat out of the garbage.

The news, political debates, financial reports from the BBC: these aren't shows that interest you. Why would you watch that? You're too busy watching that reality show about little people who get drunk in bars and beat each other up. That's way more fun.

Getting dressed in the morning is fun, too. They don't stand in their closet wondering what goes with what and where they're headed. They don't think, "I might have to wear something different for a job interview than I would to the beach." They get out of bed and put on whatever they find on the floor. Crocs, shorts, shirt, done.

Maybe they sniff it real quick, not to determine if it's clean or not but just to enjoy the smell. They don't worry if they forgot to shower because you can't worry about something you never thought about in the first place.

There are lots of successful dumb people. A lot of athletes are dumb in the best way. You can't be out there worrying about what's going to happen if you throw the wrong pitch. You just spit on the ground, rub your hand on your nuts, grip the ball, and throw it with all your might. They don't overthink, they carry on.

Being dumb keeps your mind clear and can help you be a great actor, a politician, or president of the United States.

If I'm going to be the new Dalai Lama, I'm going to have to teach people to live in the moment if we are going to get the most out of life. Well, who is more capable of doing that? Someone whose brain is filled with facts or someone whose brain is filled with Silly Putty?

The next time you're talking to someone and they toss out some statistics about global economics, don't feel bad about yourself. You're not inadequate or uneducated. You're not lazy and incompetent. You are Zen.

Om.

LET'S GO BACK

Let's go back to that big house we had off campus. The one hidden off the main road by the tall pine trees. Where the cars behind us had no idea why we were stopping and would honk at us every time we pulled into the driveway.

Let's park by the garage off the back of the house and walk across the concrete patio filled with firewood, empty beer cans, and pizza boxes, through the broken screen door, into the kitchen. Do you remember that old kitchen? We rarely cooked and yet there was still a permanent stack of horrid dishes in the sink and empty glasses stuck to the counter.

Let's go back to that old Victorian house with the oddly placed fireplaces and the added-on sunroom. I always thought that it would've been nice for a family, but looking back, I realize we were just a different kind of family. We were a family of college kids fueled by marijuana, beer, and freedom. It was an organic frat house put together by nothing more than friendship, without any affiliation to anything or anyone but ourselves.

This wasn't a house in a row of college dwellings. This small New Jersey school didn't spread out into the neighborhood. We had to seek this spot out, a good fifteen minutes away from campus where normal suburban people lived. We weren't so normal.

Let's go back.

Let's go back to choosing one of the four proper bedrooms or the makeshift few in the basement, depending on who needed a place to stay. We got the good rooms, across from each other, upstairs away from the scrum.

Do you remember our landlords? The two middle-aged sisters living next door with their mother? They didn't bother us much but they must have known what we were up to. I think they just liked having young men around or they would have complained about the loud music and the constant smell of marijuana.

There was so much weed. Always weed. It seemed like every discussion had something to do with who had time to smoke, who wanted to smoke, or who had any smoke. Remember when Dan decided we should grow our own upstairs in the large closet off the bathroom? It worked, but what were we thinking? It was New Jersey. In 1988. One visit from the police and we were done. I guess we weren't thinking much at all and that's why it was so much fun.

Let's go back to all that laughter. Hard, constant laughter. The never-ending jokes and friendly abuse and comedies on TV and videocassette. Pryor, Carlin, and Kinison. *Caddyshack, The Blues Brothers,* and *Raising Arizona.* We stretched out around the living room on couches and the floor, surrounding the coffee table that was overflowing with cigarettes, food containers, and empty cans. Discarded bills and books were buried under mountains of stems and seeds.

Do you remember how little money we had? How with all those people there were times when we still couldn't come up with enough to buy food? And still we made do. Like the winter when we had nothing but a bag of onions and found, from a book called *The Frugal Gourmet,* a recipe for "onion cinders," which consisted of rolling an onion in tinfoil and putting it in the embers in the fireplace. It was so awful and so oddly great.

You always sat in your favorite seat on the end of the sofa under the antique lamp. You were stronger than all the others, even though you were half their size. No one dared take your spot. You were the arbiter of cool in a group of insecure wanderers. We always looked to you to figure out what movies were truly good, what comedians were breaking new ground, and of course the music.

Jerry Garcia, Jorma, and Joni Mitchell. Public Enemy, the Red Hot Chili Peppers, and the mighty Neil Young. And Bob Marley, always Bob Marley floating through the hallways, mixing and spinning and harmonizing with the soundtrack of our laughter as you scanned *The Village Voice* and made plans for what concert we would be seeing next.

Let's go back to the night we saw the Grateful Dead in Hartford and Mike's friend couldn't get into the show. Remember when he came back to the hotel room at three in the morning and told us that Jesus had given him a car?

He wandered the city high on mushrooms until a valet pulled up with a car and mistook him for the owner. Not understanding what was happening, he simply said, "Thank you," got in the car, and drove away.

We thought his story was crazy until we walked him to the parking lot to put the keys in the glove box and call the owner and the only thing in the car was a crucifix hanging from the rearview mirror and a religious cassette playing through the speakers. Suddenly, Jesus giving him a car wasn't so unlikely.

Let's go back.

Let's go back and see the girls. The beautiful girls. Mine was a brown-eyed freshman acting student, while you fell for Jen. The other guys didn't understand, they saw a potential girlfriend as an intruder who would ruin our camaraderie. While they weren't entirely wrong, who could deny their friend an experience like that?

Remember when we all went to the beach and lay in the sand until the sun baked every last drop of water off the skin of our healthy young bodies before we got lost on the long walk home in the growing dark?

And while the girls came and went, and all the classes were passed, and we found jobs to earn just enough to quit, we always had the house to come home to.

At least for a while.

I wish we had the ability to see in the moment what our memories will tell us in the future. That this house, at this time, was more important than we could have known. It's hard when you outgrow something you love. It's even harder when you lose the people who came with it.

After graduation you had such definitive plans, and they were really starting to happen. You were on your way to becoming a chef on Martha's Vineyard. I still see you tearing lettuce into that large wooden bowl when we were making dinner. I see you laughing at me when I couldn't chop the vegetables the right way and threw away the herbs by mistake. I see you seasoning and stirring the jambalaya with a newfound confidence.

I would give anything to go back. Back before I received that horrible phone call when they told me I'd never see you again.

Let's go back.

Not for all of it. Just give me the end of that one night.

The night I came home late from rehearsal at school. It was cold out. The house was so dark and quiet. You were the only one still awake, sitting quietly in the lamplight, in your spot on the couch, reading Kafka.

I sat next to you with my boots up on the table, the cold still sticking to my jeans. We smoked a little, trying not to wake the others, but then I made you laugh. It was a strong, hearty laugh that overtook us and caused us to lose control. Knowing that we should have been quieter only made us laugh harder. We were breathless and we just couldn't stop. We didn't want to stop. And really we didn't have to. Not on that night. This was our place. This was our time. And no one could stop us.

Not yet.

HAVE YOU EVER ENJOYED DINNER IN A GAS STATION FOOD MART MUCH MORE THAN A MEAL IN AN EXPENSIVE FIVE-STAR RESTAURANT? I HAVE…

7-ELEVEN HEAVEN

Do you doubt that we are living in an amazing time? Do you feel like all the good things have come and gone? Well, maybe you're focusing on the wrong things. Take a break from worrying about the big, seemingly unsolvable problems and rejoice in the little things. Like the fact that you live in a world filled with 7-Elevens.

There was a time, not too long ago, that if you had a hankering for some eats, you had to get on your horse and ride into hostile territory. You'd load up your gun, shoot something, skin it, dry it, and hope it didn't give you worms. But now there are stores all around the country crammed with everything you could ever need or want, just waiting for your arrival like delicious outposts on the modern-day prairie.

The 7-Eleven is your friend. It isn't here to con you, it's here to satisfy you. Keep your fancy three-hour dinners and your white linen tablecloths. There are no waiters here.

There aren't even tables. Who needs a table when everything you buy in a 7-Eleven can be eaten while standing up?

This isn't the time to worry about finding real food. You want healthy, real food? Go to a farmers market. You want to eat off the land? Go to Idaho and hang around a potato farm. But if you want guaranteed, instant gratification that will smack you right in the mouth, head to 7-Eleven.

Everything here is perfectly processed. They aren't leaving anything to chance. This is a collection of "food-like" items that have all been engineered to bring you the exact right amount of sugar, fat, and salt to make your head explode like a shaken Dr Pepper.

And 7-Eleven doesn't mess around with the B-list of the snack world, either. These are the snack all-stars; these aisles are filled with Doritos, Fritos, and seven types of Pringles. They've got all the gum you could ever chew. You say you're looking for candy? How about Butterfinger, York Peppermint Pattie, Milky Way, and Snickers? And every new experimental version of Reese's Peanut Butter Cups you could ever want to try. If a new type of Oreo comes out, they have it on the shelves before it leaves the factory. I never even knew there were that many types of beef jerky. I think the Slim Jim people created their company just so they could hang out with the people at 7-Eleven. It may say 7-Eleven on the sign, but inside this is the Cooperstown of snacks.

This is about tearing open a package and stuffing your face. Sure, you may be able to find an apple somewhere in the back under some coffee lids, but even that will be wrapped in plastic because they don't want you to miss out on the wonderful feeling of unwrapping something. That small but potent feeling of anticipation that feels like there might be a gift inside.

The fruit people should take note. If you want us to enjoy an apple or a pear, make it look like something special. Wrap it up like a bag of Doritos, with cool labels and exciting new flavors. Apples are boring, but if you tell me I've got to try a bag of new Cool Ranch Apples, or Nacho Cheese Apples, I'll tear that sucker wide open.

Do you understand how lucky we are to live in a world that has a Slurpee machine? *The* Slurpee machine. What special type of heaven is that? A giant machine constantly churning up frozen soda concoctions just for you. What a world! While you're out there toiling away at your job, working out, worrying about not working out, the Slurpee machine is hard at work. The Slurpee machine doesn't take vacations. The Slurpee machine doesn't call in sick. The Slurpee machine has a job to do and it does it well. Who else will do that for you? Your friends will let you down. Your family will gossip about you. But the Slurpee machine has got your back.

Are you low on cash? Are you eyeing up that three-dollar hot dog but you have only two? No problem. Come on up to the register and get yourself a scratch-off game. Who else gives you a chance to win more money to get more snacks? Not those stuffed shirts at Nordstrom. Scratch away at the Vegas Slots game and you may be walking out with two hot dogs, a Little Trees Air Freshener, and some Big League Chew. The 7-Eleven wants you to win. Not just today but for the rest of your life.

Maybe you're having so much fun that you don't want to leave. I understand. Don't. You feel like loitering? This place was built for loitering. Loiter in your car and flip through your new copy of *MAD* magazine. Or better yet, sit on the hood of your car like those cool kids in *The Outsiders*. They were total loiterers. And they smoked cigarettes.

I've never been a smoker, but if I were, 7-Eleven would be the cool friend who slipped me some smokes. They love tobacco there. They've got a giant wall of cigarettes, cheap cigars, and pouches of chewing tobacco. Get yourself a giant soda and a can of chew.

Down the soda and spit your runny tobacco juice into the empty cup. Now ye're living. If you're really cool, you'll sit on the curb out front with the rest of the cool kids.

I know you're a little frightened of them when you make a late-night milk run, but don't be shy, maybe you'll make some friends. There are a lot of interesting people who sit on the curb out front of the 7-Eleven. Do they have drug problems? Maybe. Will they steal your wallet if you look the other way? Sure. But they all have a story to tell, and while that story may be filled with lies and spittle, you know one thing: it won't be boring.

And how about the guy who works at the 7-Eleven? Are you craving a real sense of community? Do you miss the days of going to a store and knowing, without a doubt, that you will see a familiar face? Then head to 7-Eleven. That guy is always there. And he always has been. Like the caretaker at the Overlook Hotel in *The Shining*, he's always been the shopkeeper there. Zoom in on a black-and-white shot from the day it opened and there he is, standing in front of a wall of cigarettes with a smile on his face.

I'm telling you, this is a great time to be alive. Despite the troubles in the world, it's nice to know that there's a place waiting to give you a quick American fix. Just waiting to satisfy your childhood desire for a sleeve of Nutter Butter or a Charms Blow Pop.

And you don't have to tell anyone you're going or share any of the stuff you bought. This is just for you. No one has to know that you stopped in for a Chipwich on your way to their lame dinner party. You don't have to tell anyone that you have a secret stash of Chex Mix in your glove box. The only person who knows is the guy behind the register and he won't say a word.

SAFE TRAVELS

You probably don't travel as much as I do, so let me take the time to give you some tips on how to fight off crippling depression, when you're away from your family, that can lead to overeating, drug and alcohol problems, and watching too many Nicolas Cage movies.

The reason travel is stressful is because it's a nonstop process of decision making. What time do we leave? Where's the hotel? How do you turn this lamp on? Is that a bug or a hair? So you have to do your best to cut down on these decisions if at all possible.

The start to your trip, the car to the airport, is a perfect example. I can't go to bed at night worrying about waking up in the early morning and trying to find a ride. I'm not wandering out in the dark looking for a cab or hoping that an Uber driver decided to get up early or, worse, is still driving because the cocaine wouldn't let him get to sleep yet.

You have to arrange the ride way in advance with a car service that probably costs an extra seventy-five dollars, but it's worth it. I'm not stressed, I'm not worried, and I'm not in danger. I can find a way to make another seventy-five dollars. I'll have a harder time making my flight if it takes an hour to find a cab that eventually drives off the side of a bridge.

I set the appointment, I give them my credit card, and explain that the 5:00 A.M. pickup that I just arranged really means 4:55 A.M. That's key. The car waits for me. I don't wait for the car. Waiting for anything is just more time to worry. Ever wait for a date to show up? It's misery. You worry if they lied to you, if they like you at all, or that maybe you're so ugly that no one will want to go out with you ever again.

No waiting! This is the same reason why we're not taking one of those airport shuttles that picks up fifty other people. If you don't have a job or any sense of urgency in your life, and you're looking for new friends, go ahead and enjoy the van. If you have any sense of urgency at all, never get in a van of any kind. Not the one to and from the airport hotel, not the one at the car rental counter, and definitely not one driven by a circus clown. No vans!

And they have to send a normal sedan. I can't worry about what kind of car they'll be driving. I'm about to fly in the sky in a machine filled with jet fuel. I really don't need to risk my life on the way to the airport in a broken-down Honda Civic from the 1980s.

The final straw was when I called one of those shady car services in New York in the beginning of my career. There I was, waiting on the sidewalk with my luggage, when a gigantic station wagon from the 1970s pulled up. At first I thought it must be a mistake. Why would a thirty-year-old monstrosity used to cart families around before they knew how to make minivans be taking me to the airport? But it was not a mistake. It was a stupid, enormous, gas-guzzling machine that was so old, the paneling was peeling off the sides. It no longer had a tailpipe, so the exhaust just billowed from holes throughout the entire undercarriage, which made it look like a ghost vehicle appearing out of a scary, foggy night.

The spooky driver, who was on the border of asphyxiation, had a long beard and big yellow eyes. He gripped the steering wheel with his skeleton hands, staring straight ahead as if he were there to drive me to the underworld rather than JFK.

It's a good idea not to accept rides from frightening men who may or may not already be dead. They have no incentive to drive safely. It's like expecting a ghost to brush his teeth. What's the point?

After surviving this death ride, I promised myself that from then on I would always use a proper car service. It didn't matter that I was poor and on my way to make a hundred dollars for a weekend of shows and the car service cost twice that. I was safe. I was on time. And I wasn't worried.

And the same goes for hotels.

A good way to stave off depression and suicidal thoughts is to try and stay in places that are at least as nice as where you live.

Checking into a fleabag hotel that's worse than where you normally sleep isn't a vacation, it's a punishment. Your bed at home isn't filled with strange curly hairs and bedbugs, so why would you pay for a place that is?

It doesn't always work out. Even if you try your best, sometimes you're in a weird spot with limited options. A town where you're lucky if they have a traffic light, let alone a three-star hotel. Like the weird cactus town I was stuck in outside of Albuquerque, New Mexico.

If it's a nice hotel, even a solid chain hotel, they welcome you with a smile and try to quickly and efficiently take care of the paperwork and get you to your room. What you don't want is someone who peeks out from the office as if he weren't expecting anyone and greets you by saying, "Hold your horses, just let me put my pants on."

This was one of those places. It was hard to tell where his nose hair ended and his mustache began. He had to blow the dust off the credit card machine because apparently I was the only customer who wasn't paying in cash and was checking in under his real name.

Another weird sign is any hotel that still uses a metal key. It could be a quaint touch in an adorable boutique hotel. In a motel in Albuquerque it's a sign that you might be stabbed in your sleep.

The white curtains in my room were yellowed from cigarette smoke. Cigarette smoke that in most places is illegal but here seemed to be encouraged based on the multiple ashtrays they provided.

The heating/air conditioning unit was one of those attached to the wall that pretends to have multiple settings but really has only two: loud and louder. There was an old ice bucket, with two glasses alongside it, topped with white paper lids, as if that's all that would be needed to stop the Ebola virus in its tracks.

Why do they even have ice buckets anymore? It's a relic from another time, when people didn't have home refrigeration. Guests would check in, unpack their traveling cocktail kit, and mix up a couple of gin fizzes with all the free ice they could scoop up. The only reason to use an ice bucket in this place is if the drug dealer in the next room gets angry and beats you and you need something to keep the swelling down.

The artwork on the walls was a bad Georgia O'Keeffe knockoff that removed all the subtlety of the floral innuendo and just looked like a giant red vagina with an eye in the center that was leering at me from across the room.

The noise truly is the real killer in these dumps. For some reason these places always sound like they're under construction or more likely under repair, as they try and clean the blood off the carpets and spackle over the bullet holes.

I could hear everything through these paper-thin walls, as if the owner tried to get away with the cheapest material he could find. I bet if the city let him, he would have separated the rooms with used shower curtains.

The housekeeper in the next room must have been blind. She was vacuuming the room as if the only way she could find the edge of the carpet was by slamming the vacuum into the wall. Bam, bam, bam! The only thing that stopped it was when I heard hangers crashing around, which could have only meant that she had gotten stuck in the closet.

When she was done I quickly missed her because her vacuuming was the only thing drowning out the coughing seemingly coming from every other room.

Is it me or does there seem to be a coughing epidemic in this country? It used to be normal to hear a cough or two, but these days whole planes full of people are hacking and honking away. People are coughing like geese all over the place, and no one covers their mouths. There was a guy next to me at the car wash recently who was coughing like he was trying to bring up his insides and shoot them straight across the room.

The hotel marketing people never think to advertise the thickness of the walls, but that would be the best thing they could do. "Stay with us—you won't hear a burp, fart, or cough that you didn't make yourself."

The moments in hotels like this, sitting on the end of the

saggy bed, listening to drug deals and belches, are the moments where I think that every choice I've made in my life has been wrong.

I had one of these moments in London, Canada. I was looking hopelessly out the window and wondering where it all went wrong. It was in a small western city in the middle of the winter and I was feeling as low as I ever had in my adult life. I looked out the window and thought to myself, "Whatever I've done that has led me to this place, at this time, was a horrible mistake."

The internet wasn't working, so I called down to the front desk. They quickly sent a bellman with keys to a new room two floors above. As we rode in the elevator, he told me that I was lucky because everything from the tenth floor up had been newly renovated. He opened the door and there was new bedding, clean carpets, and a bigger bathroom. Everything was new: the TV, the phone, and the internet hummed along at supersonic speed.

After he left I looked out the window at the very same view I'd had two floors below and thought to myself, "Whatever I've done that has led me to this place, at this time, was really worth it."

So treat yourself. Travel doesn't have to be difficult; as a matter of fact, it can be a lot of fun. When you were a kid being dragged along on trips, you had to beg for ice cream or to swim in the hotel pool. Well, now you can do any of these things anytime you want. You're the boss, the parent, and the travel agent. So get yourself a bucket of KFC, sit on the bed, and watch whatever is playing on HBO. Or better yet, order a movie—order *two* movies—throw in a room service ice-cream sundae, and enjoy the trip.

HAVE YOU EVER BEEN NEXT
TO A GROWN MAN WHO
WAS CRYING ON A PLANE
AND WHEN YOU LOOKED
OVER HIS SHOULDER YOU
REALIZED HE WAS WATCHING
SPIDER-MAN?
I HAVE . . .

PLEASE LOWER YOUR VOLUME

Some of the greatest moments in life are the smallest. Little moments like pushing open an old wooden door on a cool morning and settling into a peaceful coffee shop just after it opens. These welcoming yet tranquil moments are important. They allow us to quietly participate in, and enjoy, the world.

But these moments are becoming more and more rare because rude, inconsiderate people are ruining them.

I'm sitting in a hotel lounge where they serve breakfast. It's a beautiful space in New York with a mix of comfortable couches with low tables. Soft music bathes everyone as they speak in hushed tones, coming to life, creating, engaging, and beginning the day. It's grown-up, elegant, and down-to-earth. It was just ruined.

It was ruined by the same people who are ruining everything, everywhere I go. On flights, subways, movie theaters, ball games, anyplace where people gather together, people are showing up with their smartphones and iPads and turning their volume on full blast. They have no regard for anyone but themselves. They don't think for a second that they are being loud, that they aren't the only people in the room. They must be stopped.

This family just sat down across from me and they are a loud, disgusting noise show. The dad has an iPad—no earbuds. The younger kid has a phone the size of a frisbee—no earbuds. They are yapping away at each other, playing their devices on full volume, and they don't think this is a problem. They don't think this is bad manners. They have no regard for the man sitting across from them in silence, typing away, obviously trying to concentrate on something and writing a mean essay about them.

What the hell?

Look, we are human beings. When we show up we make noise. We talk, laugh, and chew. All natural. All forgivable. What is not natural is walking in with an electronic device and playing your annoying video like it's *The Avengers* on IMAX. You might as well walk in with a drum kit and start playing the cymbals. Why not unpack a tuba and put a screaming hawk on your shoulder? Why not just open your mouth and start screaming?

If you engage in this behavior, you are destroying the world. That is not an exaggeration. You are assaulting everyone around in a vile, upsetting manner. And if you don't stop, I am going to be forced to punch you in your face and stomp on all of your devices.

Does it occur to you for one moment that the rest of us are not interested in watching something right now? Do you notice that no one else is doing this? That you are the only one? Don't you get it? Well, now you do, so please stop it.

I have work to do. That's why I came here.

Even worse than the monsters watching YouTube videos of MMA fights and blaring Taylor Swift are the dingbats who are using FaceTime without earbuds. Talking to their friend from somewhere else, on speaker! Now I've got two inconsiderate clueless nimrods in my face. I want to kill them all. This happens frequently in airports, which are already drowning in Wolf Blitzer's nonstop blathering blaring from TVs every four feet or so.

There's no way to retaliate. If I crank up the volume on my computer, they won't notice because they're engulfed in noise. They love noise. They are noisemakers.

I hate them so much.

Mostly the parents. The parents are training their horrible offspring to be just as loud and self-centered as they are. And where does that leave me? It leaves me scowling across the way, having my book be devoured by these horrible people.

No one is telling them it's wrong. It's a tough spot to put us in. It takes guts to tell someone else how to act, especially in our culture where arrogance is ruling the day. Fueled by politics and social media, the loud and rude are really having a moment. It's as if they are putting their bad behavior on display just daring someone to say something. Well, it may be buried in a book, but I'm telling you to tone it down.

To use good behavior and consider other people takes work. It takes effort. It's not easy. It's much easier to let it all hang out rather than excuse yourself and go someplace out of earshot, away from other people to do whatever it is you have to do. But that's an act of kindness.

Maybe they're just unaware. Maybe we need a teacher to stand up and yell at them. Or a law. I guess we are going to need a law. There was probably a time when people were peeing all over the place, right in front of everybody else. And some cranky guy trying to write his book had enough and started talking to other people and they came together and decided if one more person pees in front of everybody, they're going to jail.

Maybe all this constant blasting us with entertainment is affecting everyone's hearing. My uncle can't hear at all, and every time he comes over he wakes everyone up because he can't hear the TV unless it's on eleven. Maybe that's it. Maybe we have a country of people who are hard of hearing.

I had to download an ambient sound app on my phone to drown out all the chaos going on around me. How sick is this? I'm trying to cut out other people's noise by creating my own noise. They make it seem appealing. Ocean waves, wind chimes, babbling brook. There's even an app that tells you boring stories in dulcet tones until you pass out. My wife downloaded one, then put her head on the pillow and Matthew McConaughey started telling her a tale. Far from comforted, she shot right up out of bed and started laughing herself awake.

I have noise-canceling headphones. I have earplugs. Nothing really works. That's what it's come down to. I need to create more noise, my own noise, to drown out the other guy's noise. But it's still all noise. More and more noise.

In olden times all you had to do was take a walk up a hill away from the town to find some silence. It just doesn't exist anymore. I bet there are monks on silent retreat in a cave right now talking to their friends on FaceTime and blasting Kendrick Lamar.

The family across from me finally got the check. They are going to pay. They are going to leave. I'm so happy. Now, let's see who replaces them. This is how I live now, on the lookout for another rude interloper.

Recently, I stopped into a lovely country diner on my way to meet up with my daughters. I figured I would sit at a table and write for a bit in this quaint, homey place, where the entire staff looked like they could easily be your grandmother. It felt good to be doing my work, surrounded by soft-spoken Sunday-morning New Englanders.

Until it was ruined by an awful band of "dad rockers" who decided to crank their amps up to make sure that everyone within a twenty-block radius could hear their covers of Hootie & the Blowfish.

I left before the chorus.

When I'm in New York I go to Kenn's Broome Street Bar. It's a place that's been there since the 1800s. It's got a small kitchen with two cooks who crank out some of the best bar food I've ever had. There's a great, long wooden bar with a little bit of every patron in the grain of the wood. A stained-glass portrait of a Renaissance boy hangs between the bottles and seems to be smiling at the good time he sees.

It's a great setting any time of year. I've sat in there in the middle of snowstorms and watched as the city was transformed into a wonderland. I've sat there in the open windows during perfect spring days watching the traffic make its way to the Holland Tunnel and rejoiced that I had a beer in my hand instead of a steering wheel.

There are locals who have lived there for years at a time and tourists who instantly feel like they belong. There's a small TV in the corner that seems to play the Yankee game year-round, with the sound off. I love it there.

But they have made a horrible mistake. They installed a new electronic iPad-looking wall jukebox. It blasts music like a weapon nullifying the great conversations that this bar cultivates. If you look around while some horrible heavy metal is blaring from the speakers, you see all these people shaking their heads, with a hand up to their ear straining to hear at least a part of what their friend is trying to say.

I have two strategies when I go in there now. I spend whatever I have to in order to take control of the music and play nothing but Louis Armstrong, Bob Marley, and Ella Fitzgerald over and over and over.

My second strategy is to stand with a drink in my hand, pretending to be looking for music. When there's a beat between songs, I reach behind it and unplug the jukebox. The conversation picks up, the laughter fills the space, and no one notices a thing. Everything returns back to normal, and even the boy etched in the stained glass seems to smile a little broader, grateful that he can go back to quietly eavesdropping on us all.

MORE THAN JUST A GAME

If you're looking for a fun way to enjoy time with your family, try playing a board game. If you are looking for a way to reveal the darkest side of human nature, try playing a board game with my family.

It's not whether you win or lose, it's who you play with. And if you play with my family—more specifically, my wife—you better come prepared. Scrabble is her game of choice, but what you are entering is a complex psychological maze that even if you escape will change you forever.

She wins most of the time. I think she cheats.

This is a woman who is normally sweet and nurturing. She is loyal and trustworthy. But she quickly abandons all of that when the game gets pulled from the shelf. It begins with the mention of the word "Scrabble." Like a prizefighter getting ready in the locker room, she starts to pace back and forth. She boils some tea. She picks her chair. And she sizes up the competition.

And who is the competition? Her husband, her children, and her in-laws. Maybe a young niece or unsuspecting nephew. They may have been family a minute ago, but now they are the enemy. And they will be destroyed. This is an intense attitude for a game. The very phrase "play a game" means nothing to her. We all come to the table with some popcorn, a Diet Coke, and maybe some nighttime candy. We are there to play. We are naïve. We are going to get hurt.

It's hard to explain, but she seems to change physically. She sits higher. She grows taller. She seems to turn up all of her senses. She sees better, hears more, and smells fear. Her eyes change into the eyes of a hawk. They somehow get smaller but become clearer and create a sense that she may not have a soul.

She always keeps score. Cheaters always do. We'll be settling in at the table, joking around, and like a schoolteacher reining in a class of unruly fourth-graders, she taps her pencil on the board and asks for our names as if she is meeting us for the first time. As we tell her our names, she snickers and writes them down.

"I'll go first!" my eight-year-old niece cries out.

"Wrong. Those aren't the rules," says my wife, correcting her with a quick rundown of how things are going to go. "We each pick a letter. Closest to 'A' goes first and we go clockwise from there. Got it?"

My niece is fighting back tears.

This seems like a fair, routine way to establish the playing order, but to my wife it is the first chance for victory. She usually picks an "A" or something very close to it, probably a tile that she stashed in her pocket when we were getting snacks. And while she won't pump her fists at this point, she will mutter under her breath a firm and audible, "Yes. Nice one, Nadal." When she's winning she calls herself Nadal.

There's something about the way she picks the letters out of the red velvet Scrabble bag that creates a mocking sound. Somehow the *click-clack* of wooden tiles hitting each other creates a sort of Morse code that is delivering the message to all of us that we're doomed. I also think that she's giving us all the finger. This can't be seen through the bag. I never asked her about it. But I can feel it.

Once she's picked her seven letters, she never just passes the bag, she tosses it on the board in the same way an angry customer puts the money on the counter to make the cashier pick it up. It's not a big move, but it's a move meant to intimidate us. Like a boxer tapping gloves at the beginning of a fight just a little too hard to let his opponent know he's already started beating your brains in.

"I go first, which means I go over the center star for a double word score," she says. "Right. Off. The. Bat."

We all exchange looks. Her popularity is waning.

Every house has its own rules. Little decisions that were made by the family about the fuzzy details that maybe aren't so spelled out in the rulebook. If the house decided early on that we are going counterclockwise, then that's the way it's going to go. No need to pull out the rulebook. We're all friends here.

"It says right here, in the official rules, that we go clockwise." My niece gets up to leave. We beg her to stay.

After my wife puts down her first word, records her score, takes the next letters, and gives us all the finger, it's my turn to go. It's casual. We're just getting started. I like to take my time and look for a funny word to get things going. Until my wife takes out the plastic hourglass and bangs it down on the table.

"Hey. I'm going, I'm going."

"Yeah, you are," she says, pointing at the timer.

There's a casual house rule that we flip the hourglass only

when someone is taking a really long time and we need to help move things along. My wife's rule is that it gets flipped on whoever's turn it is besides hers.

"What? You can turn it on me. It's in the rules."

I come up with a three-letter word with lame letters, something like "too." She laughs and writes down a three.

It's my niece's turn. She's eight. She has a limited vocabulary. She could use some help. My mother leans in. My wife corrects her with a loud fake cough. That's not going to happen on my wife's watch. My niece puts down a word, probably misspelled.

"I challenge."

"What?"

"That's not a word. Pick it up or I challenge." My niece, not used to being directly challenged by an adult, slowly takes back her tiles.

Now, to say that my wife is the only one with strange behavior is not fair. She definitely instigates and stirs things up, but over the course of the game everyone's bad behavior is revealed. It's like playing a game with a family of Incredible Hulks.

Everyone is driven by rage to the point that an uncontrollable ID flares up.

My mother comes for a good time, ends up confused, and gets angry when everyone grows impatient. My father doesn't like games at all but after being made to play by his wife is now physically poking everyone and has grabbed the hourglass and will now be controlling it and trying to tap the sand down faster in order to "get this shit over with."

My brother-in-law is drinking Scotch like it's water and has forgotten how to spell, all while my wife is tossing out words like a robot that has been programmed to use nothing but triple word scores. She knows the game better than anyone.

She understands that Scrabble is not just a fun word game where everyone takes their turn and comes up with creative words. If you are playing to win, there is a lot of strategy involved mostly around landing on or blocking the coveted spaces on the board.

As my niece puts out her pieces she's heckled by Cynthia: "I wouldn't do that if I were you."

"Why not?"

"Well, you can, but you're setting Jerry up with a triple word."

"So?"

"So?! So you don't know what he has. I think he has a 'Z' and if you just hand him a triple word score, he'll take the lead."

My niece lowers her gaze at the board, but I can see that she's doing some math of her own. She's thinking, "So what if Jerry takes the lead? Who's he taking the lead from?"

"You can still take it back," urges Cynthia.

"Nope. I'm good."

My wife glares at her. It turns out that Jerry does have something. He's frantically rearranging his tiles and looking right at that triple word space. He's practically drooling his Scotch on the board. My wife is irate but my niece is not fazed at all, happily munching on a gummy worm without a care in the world. She seems to be winning in her own way already.

While Jerry is Scotch drunk, he's not so inebriated that he can't come up with "zoo" on a triple word score, which he did and it gave him like a zillion points.

Cynthia slams the table.

Jerry tries to stand up in victory but is too drunk to realize this isn't the end of the game. Cynthia is not done. Not by a long shot. Jerry staggers back down and burps.

This game becomes excruciatingly slow near the end. It's my turn again and that's when things really get ugly.

My wife takes the hourglass back from my father and slams it on the table, eyeballing me the whole time.

"What did I do?"

"It's in the rules."

"Well, you don't have to be so aggressive about it," I add.

I don't know if it was because I was tired or that I didn't like being bullied, but I felt something had to be said.

"You know what's also in the rules? That it's illegal to look at someone else's letters."

"I didn't look at anyone's letters."

"How did you know Jerry had a 'Z'?"

"I did have a 'Z'!" Jerry exclaimed.

"What are you saying?" she asked.

"I'm not saying, I'm asking. How did you know?"

"Because I pay attention."

"To a drunk guy's letters when he isn't looking?" Jerry burps again and passes out.

"You're running out of time."

Here's where things got really ugly. There are certain words that are technically words but in my board game opinion aren't real words. Two-letter affairs that give the player the ability to spell a word with a "Q" without a "U." Words like Qi, Ze, and Jo. I don't like the use of these words, I can never remember what they are, but I know she uses them, so I guess and put one out.

"That's not a word," Cynthia says as she smiles.

"Yes, it is."

"I'm going to challenge."

"Fine."

Out comes the dictionary.

"I'm going to bed," my father says as he knocks the hourglass over.

"Me too," follows my mother.

My niece is asleep with her face in her gummy worms.

My wife flips through the dictionary like it's evidence.

"Aha!" she screams.

Jerry bolts up, terrified, and knocks the entire Scrabble board in the air. Tiles go flying everywhere. Hours of intense game play has been diminished to a meaningless pile.

"No!" she screams.

"I win!" says Jerry.

"You don't win."

"Yes, I do. If anything happens to the board, you go by whoever has the highest score. House rules."

My wife punches him right in the chest, grabs a gummy worm, and storms off.

I think Jerry made that up. As far as I can tell, everybody loses. Not just today but any time we play. It always ends this way. Until next time when we play dominoes, and that's a game where my mother turns into a beast from hell.

TIME FOR DINNER

We—meaning my wife and two daughters—eat dinner together at the kitchen table every night. I didn't realize this was an unusual thing until my children went to school, became friends with other kids, and came back with stories about what goes on in their households.

There are reports of everyone in the family doing "their own thing." Grabbing food by themselves, going off to their own rooms, eating whatever they can find, and going to bed without seeing each other for days at a time.

So, why exactly are you living together?

The main reason we demand that everyone show up at the kitchen table is because I want to see their faces.

"I want to see your face" is my response to most questions my kids ask: "Why do we have to watch TV together?" "Why do we have to come with you to the barbecue?" "Why are you in my room?"

"Because I want to see your face."

And I do. I understand that everyone needs alone time, when they need to be by themselves, away from the family so they can do whatever it is they want to do without their parents or siblings bothering them. I get it. But if I want to see your face, I don't care what you want.

How are you going to know if your kid is acting like a weirdo? How are you going to know if they're drinking? Or sad? Or dyed their hair purple?

By sitting down to dinner.

You want to know what mood your kids are in? Eat dinner with them.

Want to see how healthy they are? Watch them eat. If they are poking around at the peas with bloodshot eyes, you've got a problem.

Why would you not eat together? Because the kids think it's weird and it's uncomfortable being looked at? Yeah, *exactly*. What do you think the rest of life is going to be? Weird and uncomfortable. Where else are you going to learn how to pretend to be engaged in a dinner with people you don't feel like talking to? At home with your family.

Eating dinner together is when we take care of the family business. We sit around the table like we're board members of this giant corporation we are running. We discuss how things are going in the company. We get reports about lightbulbs that are out, toilets that need fixing. We bring up our schedule for the year. That's when we plan out where we're spending the holidays, who's coming over, and who has to sit next to Uncle Ken.

We share reports from the satellite offices, what's going on at cousins' homes, we tell jokes about Grandpa. We hear about boyfriends and girlfriends and rumors, and through this the children learn who they're allowed to dump on.

Sometimes there's a complete breakdown and we will laugh harder than we can remember as one of the kids gets up and decides to share her new dance or her imitation of Mom when she takes a photo on her smartphone.

Sometimes we don't talk at all, when the only sounds are the fork hitting the plate and unusually loud swallowing. That's okay. I just want to look up and see them and have them see me and realize we're family.

That's why we eat together.

How are your kids going to know you love them when you don't feed them their favorite dinner? If you don't make home-made sourdough waffles for them on Sunday? If they don't help you when you're about to flip the frittata from the pan to the plate? Pancakes aren't just a breakfast item, they're a greeting card to your children that say you care.

If you don't cook for them and sit with them and give them someone to talk to, you cease being their parent and turn into a strange roommate they share a refrigerator with.

There are rules, like no getting up early and leaving the table. There are no phones at the table. Everyone helps clean up. But mainly it's fun. We have "Waffle Week," when we have to eat a waffle every day, in a new way, all week long. We have breakfast for dinner. Sometimes we make it simple and eat plain pasta with peas.

Sometimes we don't make it at all.

And of course there's bread. There's always bread.

I'm sure it's easier telling kids to fend for themselves and not seeing them. But it's also easy to lose track of each other, and before you know it they've gotten their own apartment and moved out with no memory of you at all.

If this sounds old-fashioned, that's great. Some other weird things we do from another era: We make them come with us to the food store. We make them keep their bedroom doors open.

We make them come with us on vacation. Sundays are family day, with very few exceptions. And they're never allowed to fall in love, get married, and leave us. I'm not sure how long that one is going to last.

DON'T OPEN THE MAIL

Nothing good ever comes in the mail anymore. Gone are the days when you'd get a friendly letter from that old college buddy. There are no more love letters showing up with lips imprinted on an envelope scented with perfume. Now, there's nothing but terror shipped in an envelope by strangers plotting your financial ruin.

They say the mail is slow. Yeah, slow like a sneak attack. While you're going about your life, making margaritas with friends and shopping for a pet hermit crab, thinking everything is fine, you have no idea that someone out there is crafting a letter for your demise. Some insurance company, bank, or credit card company that you had no idea existed is gunning for you by the U.S. Postal Service.

My fear of the mail really picked up as soon as I bought my first house. Before that I had only brushed up against the system; now I was all in and I wasn't ready. I truly couldn't believe that a bank had given me a loan in the first place. It was during the housing boom when they were giving away money to anyone with a face. I applied for a big fat mortgage *over the phone* and they gave it to me. This didn't seem right. This didn't seem like it should happen. And the world soon found out that it was all kinds of wrong.

We celebrated our first night in our new home among the boxes eating supermarket cake and drinking affordable wine. After everyone went to sleep, I lay on the couch and was overcome with panic. How was I going to pay for all this? I hadn't thought this through. There was a whole list of expenses I hadn't anticipated. Furniture costs, water bills, taxes. I had no idea that once a year the state collects a mountain of money all at once. And how would they let you know? Through the mail, of course.

I was suddenly involved in a very real and terrifying game of Monopoly, but instead of a roll of the dice, every day I went to the mailbox and picked a Chance card. Every day I was being told that I had to pay a fine to a utility or that I owed money to someone but that I should be grateful because at least I didn't have to go straight to jail.

I used to love the mail. When I was young and poor and didn't own anything, the mail was fun. Anything that came was more than I had. A card from my grandmother with a five-dollar bill in it. A Christmas card from a family we didn't even remember.

Maybe even a toy from the good people at the Cheerios company.

Not anymore. Now I get death threats from the city that if I don't pay a fine by a date that has already passed, they're going to put a lien on my house.

Now I get notices about jury duty. DMV renewal notices that are always twice as expensive as I think they should be. And how about bank statements? I have a stack of unopened bank statements because they seem to show up three times a day, and if anyone is being that aggressive, I don't want to look. It's gotten to the point where I can sense how bad the news is by the thickness of the envelope.

I dread the credit card bills. It has all the mystery of the Oscars, only you are guaranteed not to win. You will instead be shocked by how much you spent.

Every time I open my credit card statement I'm perplexed and think, "If I really spent all this money, where's all the stuff and why don't I feel better?"

Certified mail is the worst. Certified mail is mail that's so nasty that when they send it they want to make sure, in writing, that you received the bad news, just for fun.

As the expression goes, "Don't shoot the messenger," but seriously, screw the mailman. That's like saying we shouldn't be annoyed with the lady who writes you a parking ticket. He knows what he's doing.

To be honest, the mailman was never a great guy. Apparently for years the mailman was creeping around having sex with everyone in the neighborhood. We thought he was delivering packages and all the while he was looking out for husbands who were at work or fighting overseas. The mailman is a real creep. He's like the milkman who gets more action. Not that I'm giving the milkman a pass. I'm sure the dirty milkman was just as perverted but only had worse hours.

The home phone is quickly becoming as frightening as the mail. Who calls on the home phone? No one friendly, no one nice, no one looking to chat. Bill collectors, telemarketers, and your mom with news that someone just died.

The smartphone hangs in your pocket like a friend who's always looking out for you. The home phone stands at its post like a prison guard. When the smartphone rings it sounds like you won something. When the home phone rings you know it's time to get back to your cell.

An email isn't half as scary as the regular mail. It's hard to be afraid of something that you can toss in the trash with the tip of your finger. And there's no way I'm going to have any fear of mail that can't be certified.

Junk mail finds its way into your home by any means necessary. I keep an alternate email account that receives nothing but junk, but there's no way to create an alternate real-life mailbox. Archaic mailing lists left over from that one time you had a magazine subscription creates a direct flow of junk mail that never stops.

For some reason, my thirteen-year-old daughter ended up on a senior citizens' mailing list. She gets offers every day for hearing aids, colostomy bags, and updates on her AARP membership. While her sister is opening birthday cards from her grandmother, she's trying to make sense of a flyer explaining that it's never too early to pick out a mausoleum.

My wife made the mistake of donating to an animal rights cause once and now the National Park Foundation, the ASPCA, and Jane Goodall send her something every week begging for more. I secretly throw it all away. I got caught once, but she wasn't that angry. The only one she really gets mad about is if she catches me throwing out a Bed Bath & Beyond coupon. In her mind that's grounds for divorce.

The only way to not fear the mail is not to care. If you don't care that you owe people money and you don't care that the bill collectors will send harshly worded letters and the energy people will send disconnection notices, then the mail is nothing to be afraid of.

A large portion of America is built on people who don't care.

Millions live beyond their means and drive cars they can't afford and no one seems to care. Once in a while someone will go to jail or end up broke, but that seems to take a really long time.

I don't know how you can live that way. If I owe anybody anything, I can't sleep at night. Donald Trump lived for years owing millions of dollars and didn't flinch. He owed thousands of people money and just didn't pay them. I know a bunch of them from living in Jersey. They hated him and screamed and yelled about him and that didn't bother him in the least. He just went to another bank and borrowed more and more money. Can you imagine what was showing up in his mailbox?

But for the rest of us the bills have to be paid, the forms filled out, and we have to sign for the certified mail.

What a bunch of suckers.

HAVE YOU EVER BEEN WATCHING TV, HEARD A SCARY NOISE IN YOUR PLACE, AND RATHER THAN INVESTIGATE JUST RAISED THE VOLUME? I HAVE...

THERE'S A GHOST IN YOUR HOUSE

If you don't have any friends, I recommend you get a ghost.

There's a ghost in my house. He wears a trench coat and carries what looks like a machine gun from World War II. He may have returned to my house after the war and had a hard time or maybe he was killed on duty, but either way he lives with me now.

And I have a photo of him for proof.

That's right. It's on my phone right now and it's clear as day. This isn't one of those smudges that may or may not be something. This is absolutely something. My security camera snapped a picture of him walking in my office. This was on the very first day that I had installed it and the ghost and I were both caught off guard.

The camera is a simple device that you plug in and aim into the room or out your window or wherever you think there's foul play or something interesting to catch. My friend introduced it to me after he had caught an acquaintance in his apartment having sex with someone who was not his wife.

Apparently the guy had been running around complaining

about his marriage and was trying to win their mutual friends onto his side. He went to great lengths spreading a rumor that his wife was cheating on him and despite all his best, faithful efforts they may break up. While my friend was out of town he thought he'd help out by giving his poor buddy a place to stay. What the guy didn't know was that there were security cameras throughout the apartment and as soon as one of these cameras sensed movement it sent out an email alert.

My friend got a ping on his phone, checked his email, and there was a naked man scampering around his kitchen. Two seconds later another ping, and now there were two naked people looking through the refrigerator for a snack, giggling and hugging like a happy couple, and one of those people was not the guy's wife. Busted.

Naturally, I bought the same camera immediately.

I installed it in my office at home, plugged it in, and headed out on the road for a show in Denver, fairly confident that I wouldn't catch anyone naked but maybe I'd get to see my dog once in a while. I was sitting backstage waiting to go on when I got my first alert. I opened the email, checked the feed, and there was my dog, scampering around my office, looking for snacks, totally naked! It wasn't very scandalous but still very exciting. Here I was in a totally different state and I could see real-time activity in my office. What a world.

I instantly thought what a cool beginning to a horror movie this would be. I pitched it to my opening act. "A guy is away, he gets a ping, checks his feed, expecting to see his dog, and there's a man, staring directly back into the camera. An ugly man, with a scar across his face, unshaven, chewing on beef jerky. He's in the house. His family is in that house! The murderer just smiles." That's a good story. Just then I got another ping.

I opened the feed again, wondering what my dog was doing now, and I swear to you, I received the image of a ghost. A shadowy yet very clear image of a man, wearing a trench coat and carrying his weapon. It looked like a ghost. A real, honest-to-goodness ghost. Spirit-like, shadowy, and somewhat menacing. I showed my friend and he nearly passed out.

I called home immediately. It was ten o'clock at night. I was in the horror movie that I just pitched. My wife answered the phone. I yelled, "Get out of the house. It's in the house." She was annoyed and hung up.

I called back. This time she humored me and answered my questions. The family was home, but no one had been in my office. There's nothing in the office that would cast a shadow of a soldier. It's on the second floor, no reflections from the street or passersby possible. This left me with only one explanation. There's a ghost in the house! She hung up again.

When I show people this picture they freak out. Grown men shudder. Children run. One woman screamed and threw my phone across the room.

There are skeptics; there always are. People who don't believe in ghosts always believe in explanations. They sit back, eating peanuts, nonchalantly tossing out ideas of other things it could be.

"It was probably the wind, maybe a raccoon, you were probably drunk." They could be right on all of those counts, but none of it could explain away this ghost.

And to be clear, this is an amazing photo. This isn't a blur. This isn't a light that needs to be highlighted and conjured into an image of some sort. This is a photo of a man. Clearly defined and creepy as hell.

Naturally I began trying to find out more about this intruder.

Or was I the intruder? The house is fairly new, around twelve years old, so why would a ghost from 1944 be walking around in it? Well, if you saw *Poltergeist*, then you know that it's not the building, it's the land: "You removed the headstones but you left the bodies, didn't you?!"

Sure, the land has always been here, and there must have been other homes on the property before this place. I figure it was probably a modest home, and as we live in Southern California, it was owned by a struggling actor. He gets a couple of bit parts, his career is starting to gain momentum, and then Hitler ruins the whole thing. He has to give up his dream while he enlists in the army to stop the destruction of the planet, something that men back then didn't think twice about.

He's out there fighting the good fight, killing Nazis, drinking coffee out of a tin cup, maybe writing a letter home to his wife, and a bomb hits his foxhole and he's killed. He's confused, upset, doesn't want to hang around in Germany, so he makes his way back home so he can call his agent and get back out there auditioning for parts. He doesn't realize that he's dead, and he just walks around the house every day wondering why his agent doesn't call. It's very similar to what I'm doing in that very same office right now.

It's kind of comforting knowing that he's here. He's become my most reliable friend. Now, when things turn on and off without any of us having flipped a switch, we know who did it. When I hear someone whisper or see something move out of the corner of my eye and there is no one there, I know there really is.

You should totally get one.

I don't see why a ghost is such a hard thing to believe in. We have a spirit. We are spirits. We have palpable energy. It doesn't seem to me that impossible that energy can't hang around in one of those planes we know nothing about.

Not all of it makes sense. I get it. It does seem a little strange that they keep their pants on and have only one outfit. If I were a ghost, I'm pretty sure I'd be naked all the time. And it is weird how confused they seem to be. You would think that if you transcend this world, you'd have a better understanding of what's going on. They never seem to be that bright, which may be why they end up stuck in an attic for all of eternity.

I stayed in a bed-and-breakfast in Massachusetts once. These are perfect settings for ghosts because the whole thing is creepy from the start. "Here's our house, we're not using all the rooms, let's have total strangers come and sleep in our extra beds, take a shower, use our soap and towels, and before they leave in the morning we'll feed them some breakfast." That's spooky.

I had checked in kind of late. The owner had one eye, and he didn't wear an eye patch. I figured that he probably did most of the time, but it was late and in the same way that most people feel great about taking off their pants at the end of the day, he had taken off his patch. It was a curious sight and I couldn't stop staring, so I did my best to stay a little to his right, out of view.

He was a little cranky, maybe from my staring, and told me I could have my pick of the two rooms as I was the only person staying with him tonight. I suddenly felt like we were on a date.

Everything creaks in a bed-and-breakfast. The stairs, the doors, even the bed creaks. If you're an engineer, you know it's because of the aging materials in the house. If you believe in ghosts, you know it's the sound of lost souls. Either way it makes it difficult to be as quiet as possible, which is what you are trying to do when you are staying in a stranger's house.

I lay down on a bed that had a doily for a bedspread and

looked like a good place for an old lady to die. I turned out the
lamp that looked like a porcelain ship and closed my eyes. I
couldn't fall asleep. I was listening to all the weird noises and
trying to figure out if anything was a threat. I heard the wind
rustling through the leaves outside my window. I thought I
heard footsteps, but it was just the old pipes groaning and shud-
dering. And then I heard something that I could not explain.

Actually, at first I felt it. A coldness came over me. Not like
a window left open or the breeze from a ceiling fan. This was a
dank, soulless cold more like a presence than a climatic event.
And then I heard it. A woman, whispering in my ear.

"I like it here," she said.

I bolted up and turned on the ship lamp, and there was nothing there. I told myself it was the wind, but man oh man, that
was a pretty articulate wind. I turned the light off and lay back
down.

"I like it here."

Oh, come on! Was it Johnny One-Eye? Was I going crazy
from exhaustion?

What was happening?

When the owner came into the kitchen in the morning,
wearing an eye patch, he found me sitting at the table. I had
been sitting there all night long, scared out of my mind. I asked
him if anyone had ever said anything about a ghost in the house.
I expected him to turn, lift his eye patch, and say, "So, you've
met Delores. She's always doing that."

But he just poured me some warm orange juice and gave me
a little chuckle as if I were making a joke. I pressed him a little
further, but he obviously had no idea what I was talking about.
But I knew it was real. I heard it. And how could I expect him
to see it, on account of his eyes and all.

It was real. It freaked me out. And I left immediately.

But unlike that creepy wraith, my ghost doesn't give off an "I'm going to murder you" vibe. First of all he doesn't talk much, which I know is strange for an actor. He also doesn't pick up steak knives and chase the children, which is good.

I named my ghost Karl. He's kind of cranky, as all out-of-work actors are, but he has hope. I feel like he has that eternal optimism you need to survive in show business, even though he's dead. As with all actors, it takes a long time before you realize when your career is over. I hope he isn't reading this over my shoulder.

I like having him around. You really should be open to your own haunting. He's like another friend. But like all friends, he can be annoying. He thinks it's funny to hide stuff on me, but it's really not. I know, people misplace stuff all the time, but this stuff goes away and appears in the same spot a little while later. Ghosts apparently have a pretty lame sense of humor.

And again, if you don't believe that my ghost can move stuff around, I get it. I'm sure you can come up with a bunch of reasons why this isn't possible. Well, if you need proof, I also have a video.

I really do.

STAYING POSITIVE

I'm often asked how I'm able to remain optimistic despite the overwhelming barrage of bad news and pessimism. An incomplete answer is that I was born this way. I was born with the right chemical balance in my brain that gives me the ability to live on the happy side of the street. I don't have a lot of depression in my gene pool and am lucky enough to not be overcome with unexplainable waves of incomprehensible sadness.

That's doesn't mean that I'm permanently on "happy mode," but it does allow me to gather up my thoughts and forge through to a more positive outlook without the aid of therapy, pharmaceuticals, or large amounts of whiskey. That's just luck.

But my genetics is only part of it. Staying positive was a philosophy that was taught to me. It's a skill that can be learned. You can do it, too. I was taught, in no uncertain terms, that we should be grateful for what we have, that we're blessed to be alive, and that we shouldn't take life all that seriously.

This was drummed into my head by my entire family, but especially from my grandmothers. Both women lived through difficult times, under difficult circumstances with the added obstacle of being women, and emerged with an outlook on life that wasn't just honorable but helpful.

They were both first-generation Americans raised by Italian immigrants who lived in rough, poor conditions made worse by the Great Depression and World War II. These two events are so enormous that it's easy to pass them off as something we've all heard about as of course being difficult, but the consequences were beyond real and life changing. These events cultivated loss and fear and beyond all a change in how one looked at and lived in the world. They truly knew what it was like to lose loved ones to war and sickness, to worry about the future, and to go without, to go to bed hungry. This was not our version of "I'm starving" because we haven't eaten in the last twenty minutes, this was very real and mapped out their childhood.

My nana grew up in an apartment in Jersey City, full of people with their share of explosive tempers and drinking problems and men with questionable morality. My other grandmother, with very little money, raised her seven children, the youngest confined to a wheelchair, and lost her husband at the young age of thirty-eight.

There was a long list of things they could complain about, but they never did. They weren't broken or defeated. They had faith. They told us, through words and deeds, that we not only have to overcome but were supposed to laugh with our family and enjoy our lives. Anything short of that and we weren't fulfilling our duty.

We were taught to truly see the suffering of others. How there was always someone else that had it worse, was dealing with more, and if they could get by, then who were we to complain?

Never complain. Don't whine. Don't be a baby. No one wants to hear it, and how does that help? We are not a family of delirious, joy-filled dingbats. But we don't quit. We just keep on keeping on.

On the morning of 9/11, I watched from Newark International Airport, where I was about to board a flight, as the second plane hit the towers. Once the confusion settled and I realized I should return to the city, it was too late. All the bridges and tunnels were shut down, so I got a cab and headed to my grandmother's house about twenty minutes outside of the city.

When my nana, the woman who had probably seen me upset more times than even I was aware of, opened the door, I had to fight back tears. She didn't understand why I was so upset. Her first response was, "My Tommy is here!" When I asked if she saw the news, she said, "Oh, these things happen," and invited me inside.

I sat in her small TV room watching the news, trying to make sense of the world, when she came in with her coat on. "I have to go meet my lady friends for cards."

"You're going to play cards? Now?"

She looked at me with pity. "Oh, you're upset. Here, have half of my tuna sandwich. I'll be back around three."

She handed me tuna on white bread and shuffled out the door as if it were any other day. She had been through so much that this cataclysmic event was just another bad day, in a list of bad days, that we'd have to face and overcome. These things happen.

Other bits of advice I was given: "I'll give you something to cry about." "What do you have to be unhappy about? Do you know how other children live?" "It's all perspective." "Buck up."

The world is filled with pain and hardship. We all have reasons to quit. We all have reasons to look at the world and think it's hopeless. But what does that get you?

When you are traveling and there's a delay, is it going to help your situation if you get angry about it and start sulking and fighting with your fellow travelers? If you don't get the job you were hoping for or the girl or guy you wanted, what's the course of action? Climb into bed and stay there forever? Or go after another job and another lover?

Life isn't easy. It's actually extremely difficult, with only one guaranteed ending. But you should refuse to waste it, if not for yourself, then for everyone around you. That was my grandmothers' greatest trick—they weren't living this way for themselves, it was for the sole purpose of helping others. Just knowing that we have the power to make it a little easier for everyone else who is muddling through should be enough to make us try.

Try and be strong. Try and be better. Try to enjoy.

THE GREATEST SHOW ON EARTH

When I'm watching a school choir performance these days, I spend most of the time trying not to cry. In the beginning I was trying not to cry because they were so bad, but now they're simply the most moving, stirring, and emotionally packed shows I have ever seen and I've seen *Cats* at the Valley Village Community Theater, so I know what I'm talking about.

When the kids started out in nursery school and kindergarten, it was hard not to get choked up, but that was more out of pure cuteness. Those shows were tantamount to tossing a box of puppies out on the stage. You ooh and ahh and can't believe anything so cute actually exists.

Then they grow a little and awkwardness sets in and for years the shows are just horrible. There's some joy seeing your own child up there, but the rest of those kids are a mess. They can't sing, they can't dance, and anything with an instrument is a certain form of torture. I get that every kid should play an instrument, but that doesn't mean the rest of us should have to hear it. That's for their own family to deal with.

That's one of the great tests for a parent. You know that making your child practice an instrument that they can't play is doing the right thing. You know that practicing is the only way they will get better. And you also know that they're going to produce the worst sound in the world and bring it into your home.

It's like inviting your child to use a jackhammer on the dining room table in the middle of a dinner party.

Our school started the kids off with the recorder. It's a funny flutelike first step. It's not the best instrument in the world. If it were, it would come with a case, and it does not. The kids have to carry it to school in a sock. And that's okay, because you know it's not going to be around very long. No one continues playing the recorder, and no one has ever formed a band and asked if anyone knows a recorder player, but it's the gateway drug of instruments.

Anyone who shows any aptitude at all with this sock flute goes on to choose their next instrument, and this is when the trouble starts. Suddenly the grade is filled with oboes, tubas, drums, and the dreaded violin. And what are you going to do with a bunch of kids with instruments? Form a band. And what are you going to do with this band? Put on a concert and make everybody listen.

Listen to "Hot Cross Buns" and "Jingle Bells" and it doesn't matter what else because it all sounds like a clown dropping off his garbage at the dump.

Clankity metal, screeching horns, and crying children. My wife and I couldn't take it. Maybe we're bad parents, but we stopped at the sock flute and convinced them to take up dance.

My wife has been a dancer her entire life, starting as a child and later dancing professionally, so it's only natural that she makes our two daughters into smaller versions of herself. Thank God. It made for a much quieter house. And while our concerts had much better music, they were just as rough to sit through.

I always enjoyed them, but not for the right reasons. I'm a big comedy fan and these shows were hilarious. Just the idea is funny. Let's get some creatures who are growing at an incredible pace, who have no chance of controlling or understanding their bodies, put them in costumes, and make them try and dance in unison for other people.

This is about as far away from the Rockettes as you can get. These kids aren't even close to the same height, definitely not the same shape, and not nearly the same skill level. We've seen kids fall down, fall off the stage, and fall in love right in the middle of a show. It's chaos in tights.

And dance shows are long. They are *so* long. They start at ten in the morning and go until half-past everyone's bedtime. There are so many kids and so many numbers that it's just impossible to make them any shorter.

As difficult and challenging as it is for the dancers, it is equally as hard for the audiences. I spent years watching parents nap during the show and be punched by their wives when they start to snore. I've seen grandparents smuggling alcohol into the bleachers, going out for a smoke at intermission and never coming back.

And yet as tough as they are to watch, everyone in the audience is recording every second of it on their phones. The idea that there will ever come a time when the entire family gathers around to watch a replay of this is absurd. It would be more fun watching Grandpa's colonoscopy. I'm guilty of it, too. Even though my eyesight isn't the greatest, I once spent an entire show recording my daughter on my phone, only to find out hours later that I had been following the wrong girl.

These are rough years for all involved: the budding singers, dancers, musicians, teachers, parents, friends, and relatives. Even the janitor isn't safe as we are all forced into this exercise, season after season, show after show.

And then something happens.

The children get older and they get to decide for themselves if they want to participate. They move beyond doing it because their parents said so. They do it now because they have some real passion. They care and they try and they practice on their own, out of the sight of their parents. They do it for themselves, all year long, and suddenly we get an email to save a date on our calendar because there will be a show that we didn't see coming and didn't know anything about.

And it will be a really good show. Not all of them. Not all the time. But there are moments that can take you as high as, if not higher than, anything you have ever seen because there is courage and dedication and excitement. You are literally watching a human being evolve. They are beginning to harness all that love and fear and energy of being a person and expressing it, daring to be judged.

There is nothing more hopeful. It's actually heartbreaking how hopeful it all is. And when you see them reach, see them strive for something bigger than themselves, and sometimes hit it, and they know it and the audience knows it and the teachers and the other kids all know it . . . well, that's just about the most amazing thing you could ever see.

HAVE YOU EVER TAKEN AN EXIT OFF THE FREEWAY THAT YOU KNEW WAS WRONG JUST BECAUSE EVERYONE IN FRONT OF YOU DID? I HAVE....

FOLLOW THE HERD

Sometimes you have to be your own person. You have to strike out on your own and act the way all those motivational sayings on social media or on posters at the car wash want you to act. "You do you." "Take the road less traveled." "Be the captain of your own ship."

But that takes a lot of work, which is why they have to continually yell at us like a drill sergeant about it. And while embracing your independent streak has its own rewards, sometimes you have to give yourself permission to take the easy way out and just be a part of the big stupid herd. Go to the big stores, eat from the chain restaurants, and watch *The Bachelor*. We can't all be Andy Warhol, sometimes we just have to be normal. And sometimes normal is all you need.

So do the easy thing and enjoy the nice free continental breakfast in a lobby of a Holiday Inn Express. Drink bad coffee and eat a bagel that's only a bagel because they say it is. Stare mindlessly into that rotating toaster machine and wait for that bagel to slide down the back like a dirty, crumb-filled slot machine. Scoop it up with your plastic knife and waddle back to your chair. You did it.

Will you enjoy this breakfast because it's delicious? No. You'll enjoy it because it's easy. Are there better breakfasts out there? Sure. But they're more expensive and it's a lot more work. You'll have research to do, reviews to read, and reservations to make.

The only decision you have to make today is cereal or a hard-boiled egg. You didn't stop in this hotel for some grand experience, you stopped here because you started seeing double on the freeway and needed to lie down. And before you start driving again, you need a fresh brain that isn't troubled by trying to be a better you.

Sometimes we just need the quick and easy because we don't have time for slow and difficult. An orchid needs proper sun and just the right amount of water or it will wilt and die. A weed eats and drinks whatever it can and it grows like crazy. Be a weed.

Not every moment in life has to be special. Sometimes you just have to go and get things done. Go to Walmart, get yourself some pants, some spray paint, and a big-ass box of beef jerky. Go home, microwave some pizza rolls, and watch a repeat of *Friends* followed by *Impractical Jokers* and everything on the Food Network. It wasn't a special day, but it was good enough.

And what's so special about being special anyway? Now that the generation of kids who were told they were special for no reason has become adults, I think we can all agree they turned out to be pretty entitled people. Maybe if they were a little less special, they would compromise, show empathy, and be kinder to each other.

I think it's Burger King's fault. From the moment they told us "You can have it your way," we haven't been the same. People stopped thinking about *we* and replaced it with *me*. Things were much better when the popular phrase of the day was "It's my way or the highway."

Looking for some fun? The herd loves fun. Let's go to the movies together. *Spider-Man 12*? Sure. Another *Pirates of the Caribbean*? Yes, please. Sure we know everything that's going to happen, but who cares. There will be a bad guy, he'll threaten to destroy the world, our hero will save everyone, and we'll walk out of the theater feeling like we just ate a pile of junk food. That'll do the trick. What else are you going to do? Go to an art house and read the subtitles of a depressing French film by yourself?

Not today you're not.

And make sure to stop at the counter and load up on snacks. Get the biggest popcorn they have, put butter on it, and grab a gigantic soda that takes two people to carry. Throw in some Sour Patch Kids and something really crunchy. When you're part of the herd you don't just eat, you graze and you make noise. A lot of noise. And it doesn't matter because so does everybody else and no one cares.

There's no fighting when you're part of the herd because you have to get along with everybody. You're not trying to change everyone's behavior. This is about acceptance. You want to make a phone call in the middle of the movie? Sure, why not? Everyone else is. If they don't think it's important to hear everything the Hulk has to say, why should you?

You know what else the herd does? They stand in lines. Long-ass lines, and they don't mind. So stand in that mile-long Starbucks line at the airport. Wait in another line for the barista to make your drink, wait in line for the bathroom, and then get in line at the gate with the rest of zone seven. Will they take your suitcase from you? Probably, but that's okay. It'll give you more lines to stand in when you land. There's the line at baggage claim, the line for the shuttle, and the rental car line. Mindless, timeless waiting. What a relief that you're not bothered by any of this.

And that's the key attitude to have: to not be annoyed. Understand that we are going to move a little slower in the herd. We are going to have to be a little less aggravated, a little more patient, and a little less irritated. And it will be worth it because the herd will bring us to good things. Airports, stadiums, beaches, and schools. Mardi Gras, K-pop concerts, and Times Square on New Year's Eve.

I was at a Dodgers game last night. There were 44,999 other people there, too. One giant herd. And I'll tell you something, all kidding aside, it was beautiful. It really was. All these people, different shapes and sizes, being herded like cattle into this enormous stadium. We were all there for the same reason, to enjoy a baseball game. We were going to eat the same hot dogs, the same terrible nachos in a bag, and the same flat beer, and it was glorious.

Don't tell me that there isn't beauty in that. Sure, there are some people who are a mess. There was an obnoxious woman who was yelling incoherent insults at both teams. There was a drunk guy falling all over everybody every time he got up to pee, which seemed to be five times an inning. But they were the minority. The majority of the people were having a great time.

There were all types in that crowd. There were people with so much money that they probably fart gold coins. There were young people with no money at all. There were people with bad backs and six-pack abs. Someone had herpes. Some couldn't see. Someone might have killed a guy earlier in the day. But in the stadium we were just a part of the herd watching a game.

Together.

You know what the herd does? It gets along. Don't we need a little more of that? Don't we need to all stand up and do the stupid wave simply because everyone else is doing it?

It's fun to play the dumb games together on the jumbotron. We sing along to the same songs. We cheer together and let out a collective groan and really care when someone gets hurt and applaud them when they rise up. And we cheer for the guy who catches the foul ball and we all boo the guy who dropped the easy one.

We laugh at the couples kissing on the kiss cam, the children jumping and cheering, the fat guy dancing like everybody's watching. We enjoy them because they are a reflection of us, fiercely independent and unique, while still a part of the herd.

When the game is over and we all head to our cars and sit in traffic, it seems impossible that we'll ever get home. How can all these people move at the same time and get anywhere? How can this possibly work? But it does. Because we're getting along for a moment, a little less selfish, a little more united.

Part of the herd.

HAVE YOU EVER WALKED NAKED FROM THE SHOWER TO THE DRYER TO GET YOUR PANTS AND BEEN REMINDED BY YOUR SCREAMING FAMILY THAT YOU DON'T LIVE ALONE? I JUST DID . . .

HOME ALONE

Whenever my wife and children leave me home alone I immediately think, "Now's my chance!"

It's rare to be in the house by myself with this kind of freedom. I have a wife and two daughters who are beautiful people but who stop me from doing a lot of the things I like to do. I didn't realize when got I married and had children that I was creating three wardens who would patrol the grounds and tell me what to do. But not today. There's no one here to tell me I can't, I shouldn't, or get that out of your pants. The possibilities are endless and I'm about to go party like it's 1998, the last time I was alone.

Maybe I'll smoke a big, fat, disgusting cigar. That's one of the things they hate the most. I can't really do it at all when they're home, not even outside. I mean, I could, but they hate them so much that it kind of takes the joy out of it. They dramatically close the windows and doors, and when I come back in they all scatter as if I'm carrying a bucket of manure covered in fish guts, which I'm not, it's just me.

Yeah, this could be fun. I'm going to smoke a cigar. Not inside, of course, I'll go outside. But I do have to catch a flight to Nashville tomorrow and I don't want to stink up the plane. Not that anyone would say anything to me. No one ever does. You could have horrible garbage breath and no pants on and no one would dare say a word. But still, it's just bad manners.

Oh well, I guess smoking's out. Maybe I'll arrange my shirts. I've been meaning to go through all of them. I have drawers full of shirts that I never wear. I think I wear only four shirts in total. I should get rid of the rest of them. Why am I keeping them if I never wear them? I guess I think I will one day. I have a blue denim shirt that I'm holding on to because it would be perfect for a bonfire on the beach. But who am I kidding? I don't know the kind of people who know where to go on a beach at night and who bring along all the wood and stuff. But who knows, maybe I'll meet someone like that one day and then I'll be happy that I held on to that shirt. Yeah, I can't throw that stuff away, and what am I thinking? I'm home alone, this isn't time for tidying up. I should be making a mess.

Maybe I'll just have a drink. I could make a martini or open a bottle of wine like they do in Europe. It's a little early for that, I guess. This isn't France. In the United States, drinking alone is strange, drinking alone at noon is trouble. I don't want to be hung over before my trip even begins.

Maybe I'll jump in the pool. It's a nice day. Why not? I wouldn't even have to put on a bathing suit. I could swim naked. That sounds fun. Maybe I'll eat a little something first, take off all of my clothes and jump in the pool, come back inside and fall asleep on the bed for an hour, wake up, shower, eat some more, and pack for my trip.

That actually sounds amazing. A summer nap on cool sheets is one of the really good things in life. I haven't done it in a really long time because there's always someone around. The kids don't burst into my bedroom as much as they did when they were little, but they still do once in a while, and finding their father naked in bed wouldn't be so great. Finding your father napping in bed fully clothed isn't that great either. You expect to see your dad fall asleep sitting up in the living room. That's understandable. But if he climbs under the covers in the middle of the day, that's just weird.

"Where's Dad?"

"He just went to bed."

"It's noon."

"I know. We're in real trouble. We really should open our own bank accounts and make sure we have a good supply of canned goods."

Under the covers doesn't mean you're tired, it means you're hiding from something or you're really depressed. No one wants a dad who hides, you want Dad to stand up, fight, and protect. It's his job to make you feel safe. You don't want there to be trouble at the door and look back and see your father's face poking out from under the comforter.

No one wants to see sad Dad either. Dad needs to suck it up. No one is saying Dad can't cry, but he better make it quick. The faster he wipes off those tears and returns to normal Dad face the better.

I don't have to worry about any of this today, because I'm alone and no one will see me taking a naked swim or nap. But to be honest I'm a little worried about the sun. I've never been naked outside for any length of time. That may seem weird, but I grew up in New Jersey, and it's not a place that encourages public nudity. It's actually against the law to run around naked at any time. The point is, I'm very white. Especially down there. If I go outside naked for even a minute, I could burn some essential equipment. That wouldn't make for a fun flight, night, or next couple of days.

I guess I could just go straight to the nap, but now that I think of it, a nap seems like a waste of time. I don't want to waste this kind of freedom with my eyes closed, not realizing how much fun I could have. When you're living in a house full of family, the only time you have freedom is when you're asleep, so let's enjoy this sweet moment while I'm wide awake.

Maybe I'll just work out. I really should work out. I should definitely exercise. It's too hot to go for a run, but maybe I could ride the indoor bike or lift weights. I feel like I don't lift weights enough. I should, my arms are getting soft and wiggly. But I don't feel like I have the energy. Maybe it's because I haven't eaten.

I should really just eat something already. I am hungry. I'm always hungry. I have some elk sausages in the bottom of the refrigerator. I could throw those on the grill and split them with the dog. But it seems like a lot of work for one person. I like when the family is around and I have someone to cook for. When the kids eventually move out we're going to have to invite people over just so I have someone to cook for. Cooking for two is okay, but it's really just one more than one, and cooking for one is no fun at all. Cooking for the dog isn't that great either. She eats so fast and never says thank you. Maybe I'll just eat some nuts.

But what about my work? I have so much writing to do and all those emails to go through. I really should be spending this time getting my work done, but what's wrong with a little fun once in a while? If only I didn't feel guilty about not using my time wisely. I'm so boring.

Maybe I should just be more constructive and change some

lightbulbs. I keep meaning to do that, which is another way of saying that I keep forgetting to do it but feel bad about it when I remember again. I should also put that ladder back in the garage and sweep off the top deck where it's caught all those leaves over the months that I forgot or skipped taking it back down. It's amazing how many things always have to be done around here. Lightbulbs and doorknobs and recycling. Trips to Goodwill, fences to be fixed, garages to be swept. A house is like a living thing that's constantly in need of a haircut.

This is pretty pathetic. I have the whole house to myself and I'm thinking about lightbulbs? What's happened to me? I'm trying to think of what I did before I was married with children. I did stuff. I think I did stuff. Didn't I do stuff?

Maybe I should start playing video games or take a trip to a marijuana dispensary. Maybe that would be fun. But that sounds kind of lonely. Forget it. I'll just sit here, in this empty house, and text my family once in a while.

I wonder what they're doing. And when are they coming home?

HAVE YOU EVER FISHED THE PRIZE OUT OF A BOX OF CRACKER JACK AND REALIZED IT WAS ACTUALLY YOUR TOOTH? I HAVE...

PLAY BALL!

It's a hot July day at Yankee Stadium and the seats are so scorching hot that the minute we sat down we turned into cartoon characters who had just sat their asses on a hot stove. If we were anywhere but a baseball game, we would have leapt up and planted our backsides in a bucket of ice water, but we wouldn't dare break this tradition, so the four of us settled in with our hot dogs and beer.

The bruised and battered Baltimore Orioles are in town, but still the game is sold out with more than forty-five thousand fans who are sensing that this might be the Yankees' year. That's what baseball fans always think at the beginning of the season, but this is midsummer and we're still thinking it.

I've known these three friends for most of my summers, enough that just the fact that we are still here together seems like a certain kind of accomplishment.

Every season, regardless of how busy we are, where we are living, or what kind of year we're having, we meet up, push through the turnstile, and spend the day watching baseball.

But mainly I'm here for the food.

Naturally I lose it when I'm at the ballpark and see it as my duty to eat from the first pitch to the last. Peanuts, hot dogs, sausages, ice cream in plastic batting helmets, soda, and beer. I like the ballpark nachos that aren't nachos as much as a bag of chips with some melted orange plastic that they pass off as cheese. But when they're mixed with a green outfield and the Yankee pinstripes, they're the best nachos I've ever had.

There's a long list of foods that I eat only when I'm at a baseball game. I never buy Cracker Jack in a store, but as soon as the vendor comes by I'm tossing money at him. The same with cotton candy. You'll never see me skipping down the sidewalk with a giant pink cotton candy, but if I'm at a baseball game, there's a good chance I'll have one in each hand and be chewing bubble gum at the same time.

Brian is a redhead and is suffering under this harsh sun more than the rest of us. He found a bucket of ice with bottled waters in it and dove into it up to his waist. Security had to pull him out of it, but when they saw his pale white skin they let him dive in one more time.

He has more sports knowledge than the rest of us, always has, and although he's the same age he's further along in life than us as well. He married his high school sweetheart and already has the last of his four children finishing up college. Brian is a Michigan alum and is beyond proud of his kids, especially because two went to Michigan, and the other two to Penn State and Wisconsin. Beyond education, this enabled Brian to go to many big-time football games. He's never happier than when he's in a giant stadium filled with equally rabid fans.

The new Yankee Stadium that opened in 2009 still feels like a newish apartment that doesn't quite feel like home. We're still trying to find our spot on the couch. The vast building lacks the camaraderie of the old, smaller ballpark where every seat was tucked against the next. Fans sitting behind home plate heard everything they were screaming in the bleachers. I recently read that for the first time opposing players don't mind coming to Yankee Stadium because, with the fans are far enough away, they no longer hear the insults. That's a horrible thing for New Yorkers to hear. Sarcastic, verbal torment is what we're good at. But still there's no other place we'd rather be. We'll just have to yell a little louder.

The Yankees seem to be a little lazy today except for Brett Gardner, who seems like he's never been lazy a day in his life. At thirty-six, he's the oldest player on the team but never lets up. He's lightning fast around the bases and drives pitchers crazy with tough at bats that can last over twenty pitches. He's always been a bit of an underdog, which is the type of player I like to root for, especially since I'm more than ten years older than him.

There's a Baltimore fan next to us who is much more vocal than a fan of a team that is thirty-five games back should be. But at least he's had a couple of funny lines, another thing New Yorkers respect. Truth be told, we're so far ahead of this team in the standings that we're not that invested in this game. We'd like a win, but that's not really why we're here.

Lou is a talented lawyer and I love hearing about the cases he's working on. He's a natural adviser and always has a very practical and well-thought-out point of view on things. He was the first guy I drank with as a freshman in high school, and when our parents found out, Lou showed his early legal prowess as he got us all out of trouble. He was always the brains of our operation. His nickname back then was Grandpa, which spoke to his wise and elevated stature among us wayward grandchildren.

Dave recently joined a country club and now wears collared

shirts to play golf. We never would have pictured that back in high school when he was riding around on his motorcycle, getting into fights with the arrogant upperclassmen who looked like their dads belonged to country clubs.

He says that his club is different from those other ones and that it's a lot of guys just like him. That must mean they like to drink. Dave's involved in a long love affair with Tito's Vodka. They both seem very happy.

The Yanks are really making a mess of things today. This new pitcher has let up two home runs already. They've made three errors and this lowly Baltimore team is soundly beating us. These days we all look to Aaron Judge, and even he looks sleepy. The fan behind us is getting drunker and he's not so funny anymore.

Lou bought us another round of beers. I found a short line and grabbed a bunch of waffle fries. Dave just made a crack about the Orioles to the drunk guy. Some of his high school ways are coming through, and although it may lead to a fight I have to admit that I'd like to see it.

What makes sharing this day together so great is that we don't have to get to know each other. I know things about them that no one else knows: their first loves, their failures, and all their successes. It's nice to still be with people who were actually there at your most embarrassing and ugly moments. We can all be ourselves because there's nothing left to hide.

My friends aren't perfect. Nobody is. As a matter of fact, it's the flaws that sometimes make a person more interesting. Being a friend means having the ability to let some of their bad behavior go. We can't be perfectly aligned with anyone. So why should we expect that from our friends or family?

I have friends that spit their food when they talk. I have friends who refuse to pay a penny more than what they spent on a bill at lunch. I have a friend I would probably never hang out with if I had just met him but I've known him so long he's grandfathered in.

The common thing about them all is that they're fun to talk to. We make each other laugh. And we care about each other. And that's enough. We could all do with a little more forgiveness these days.

But these Yankees have given up on this game, and that's unforgivable. The Baltimore fan got into a fistfight, thankfully not with Dave.

We've had a pretty good streak. The Yankees have won most of the games we've come to. But not today. We stumble to the subway, cram in with a bunch of other fans, and head downtown. It's time to smoke a cigar, drink some more, eat some more, and try and hang on to the clock. Slow down the time. Until next year.

It's not a mistake that we get together at a game. This is the group who we learned to play around with. We have inside jokes that are over thirty years old. We cut school, played hooky, and ran away to the beach. We learned from each other that it was important to break out of our lives for a bit and enjoy ourselves as much as possible. We knew each other as children and even now that's who we see. And that's why, all these years later, despite an ocean of responsibility, we won't be working today.

We'll be at the game.

HAVE YOU EVER BEEN SO
WIRED ON SUGAR THAT
YOU JUMPED ON YOUR
DOG'S BACK AND RODE HIM
AROUND LIKE A HORSE?
MY KIDS HAVE . . . .

GET A DOG

Get a dog. Stop your whining about life and focusing on all the bad stuff that can and does go wrong and get a damn dog.

I know, you've been thinking about it, weighing the pros and cons. Just get a dog.

I say this as someone who doesn't like hassle and doesn't enjoy having his stuff ruined. But we got one and I have been converted. Get a dog.

There's a dog under my desk right now. And she's totally annoying, growling at every person who walks up the sidewalk in front of my house, acting like a fierce guard dog protecting me from that little old lady and her Chihuahua.

We weren't going to do it. We are cat people. I like a nice cat because they fit the style of my favorite relationships. They are independent, swing in on their own, drop by for some love when they need it, and move on. But I also have children and kids want a dog. They all do. We all did. And I'm a sucker for the textbook narratives of life, so I made them a deal. When the cats die we get a dog. I was only half joking. And only one of the cats died, but they were so upset that it felt like it was time to get the dog.

There are certain decisions that you make in life, for your family, that have that extra weight. That extra little oomph. As the parents you have power. And a lot of times you wield that power in very practical ways to keep the family safe, provide for them, and all those other boring, life-sustaining things. But every once in a while you get to use your power for pure fun. You unleash a major decision based on nothing but love and joy, and the people rejoice.

And when you make these decisions, there is nothing more fun than dropping it on everybody. You sit at dinner going through the routine, and then you make an announcement: We are going to Disney. We're putting in a pool. We're cutting school tomorrow. We are getting a dog.

As you can see from the list these are limited, these don't happen all the time. If you are superrich and you try and get the same juice every year out of announcing yet another vacation to Europe, it won't happen. These decisions and announcements and proclamations have power in their rarity. These announcements are so rare and so much fun to make that I understand if you get a dog just so you can tell your family that you are getting one. I would say that telling them you are getting a dog is about 90 percent of the fun of getting one.

I love the secret parent meetings, too. In hushed tones, as if you are planning an attack on a foreign country, you hatch the plan. And then launch it on them. We told our kids at the table, which is a great place for most things. The table, where we eat and share and grow stronger. You can keep your living room with its fancy cushions and tempting movie viewing and video game playing. Keep your soft recliner by the fireside. This isn't one of those times. Give me a hard yet comfortable chair. Give me a table where we have had hard discussions and celebrated our victories. Where we have poured wine and broken bread. Where special tablecloths have been set and the seldom-used glassware came out. The table where we have meals as simple as a quick breakfast out of a cereal bowl to the most glorious of all Thanksgiving meals.

No, it is at the table where I will announce to my people that "your mother and I have made a decision. We are getting a dog."

Mayhem! Forks are dropped. Milk spit. Children rise from their chairs and start dancing around. Tears are shed. This is no longer a routine meal. This has been turned into a celebration. And it has ceased being a discussion. It is no longer a debate. We are getting a dog!

A side note, for those of you who live alone or even with one other person or even a strange roommate. You will enjoy this part of getting a dog just as much because once your decision has been made you are changing. You are different. And that difference is your heart opening up and growing just a little bit, just from making this decision. You are like the Grinch holding one of those silvery ornaments.

Now where are you going to get your dog? Loaded question, right? We all know the fierce debates and the quick judgments in making this decision, and you can come under attack for even thinking that you get your dog from one of those breeders. But frankly, I don't care. Just get a dog. If you are rich and you want one of those fancy Westminster Dog Show purebred pointers, go for it. There are good breeders, horrible puppy mills, and there are a zillion dogs out there in need of rescue and adoption. That's what we did and it's not so we can feel justified in our goodness at cocktail parties. It's just the way it shook out.

To be honest, I liked the idea of getting a golden retriever from a fancy, well-respected breeder. I would like to tell you that it was after a deep philosophical debate that I changed my mind, but honestly it was the fact that it cost five thousand dollars for one of these arrogant animals that changed my tune.

And truly, I am a mutt person. I married a mutt. I am a mutt. We're mutts! We are not purebred. Leave the golden retrievers for the Kennedys. Let the corgis run around Buckingham Palace. We got a dog that seems like she's mostly a black Lab with something else mixed in who was found on the side of the road in Bakersfield. Is our dog going to win a big blue ribbon in some dog show? No, she is not. But like any runaway in Bakersfield, you know she has a story to tell. This dog has seen some stuff. And unlike a dog that was born in a mansion, this dog is happy to be here. This dog is happy to be anywhere.

We found her on the internet. We started looking at rescue places near us. Adoption agencies. The ASPCA. All fun places to look and all with pretty decent websites that, unlike my own, are updated every day. There are current photos of the actual animal you could adopt sitting right there on your laptop. And these places are honest. They'll let you know if a puppy is crazy active or kind of shy or gets upset when it hears Barry Manilow songs.

After spending some time on these sites, we started to feel like we were on some kind of dating site. Not unlike what you do when trying to find a date, you scroll and look and think and analyze and then someone just hits you. For some reason, probably chemistry or maybe just good lighting, someone stands out and you just know. And my wife knew. She stood up from the desk, grabbed her keys, scooped up our youngest daughter, and without saying goodbye was screeching out of the driveway. I looked at the laptop and there was the culprit. A tiny black Lab puppy with love in her eyes sending a secret message for us to come and get her.

If you want to take all the decision making out of the equation, bring a child with you to the adoption agency. Within minutes of their being there we received a text of my daughter with this puppy in her lap. Holding a dog that she was never going to let go of. If we decided not to take the dog home, not only would we not be coming home with a dog but we would be living with one fewer child. She would have gladly lived in the cage with her and never seen us again.

When a new family member comes into your home you immediately are forced to do for someone other than yourself. Isn't that what love is all about? Thinking and doing for others. Rather than sitting around and thinking about your feelings and your stomach and your day, you are now rushing around grabbing blankets for a bed, picking up things that could be choked on. There is another heartbeat in the house and you can hear it and want it to be okay.

And there's nothing more fun than a trip to the pet store. This place filled with nothing more than fun stuff for animals. Squeaky toys, fun-looking ropes, things you never even thought about before. And what about a bowl? Or a little T-shirt? Or maybe a hat? Oh my God, look at this little hat with bunny ears on it. Should we get this hat? We have to get this hat!

We rescued a puppy. Great for photos. They smell great. There's nothing cuter on the planet than the baby versions of anything, and the baby version of a black Lab will just about melt you into jelly immediately. But holy cow, are they a lot of work. There is definitely something to getting an older dog.

An old dog has been around. An old dog knows where to pee and the difference between a stick and a table leg. They've been with people before and they are what they are and you can't teach them new tricks because they know their tricks and you either like 'em or you don't. And best of all, they like to sleep.

I would encourage you to get a lazy dog as well. A big fat lazy ball of fur that you have to coax outside for a walk. Bella is filled with more energy than a burning star and we can't keep up. I want a pillow with eyes. What I got was a thoroughbred horse that wants to run across the prairies.

But hey, love is work. I don't want to harp on the hardships because that's beside the point. Being married is a lot of work. Raising my children is a lot of work. But it's the kind of work that you don't think about because you are going to do it no matter what.

She has lived with us now for three years. And honestly it's only in the last year that I really got it. The affection. The joy. The squeezing her. The transformation that she has made on the house. When I'm on the road I think about my dog. I like saying "my dog." Where's my dog?

I want to travel with my dog. I want to wrestle with my dog. And squeeze her. And throw a frisbee with her. And despite all my protesting, and acting like the dog is a pain in the ass, I really am in love. And even worse, I'm thinking about getting another one.

Maybe I'll announce it tonight when we're all at the table.

HAVE YOU EVER SKIPPED TO THE END OF A BOOK TO FIND OUT THE ENDING AND REALIZED IT WAS JUST A BUNCH OF RANDOM ESSAYS? YES, YOU HAVE.

AND NOW A WORD FROM OUR SPONSOR

This is a list of all the great things out there in the world that we take for granted. A bunch of small stuff that you can have right now while you're wasting time longing for that trip to Fiji or the day you'll be able to buy a Ferrari. I have not been paid by any of these fine products, artists, or companies; I just really like them a lot and use them as rewards as I go about my days. So here's a list of favorite things:

I. DORITOS

Come on! I don't know what secret lab they have, but the Doritos people have been killing it for a long time. Are they decadent? Yes. Are they bad for you? Probably. Do I have any idea what's in them? Not a clue and I'm not asking.

I haven't eaten them with any regularity since high school, but every once in a while, when I'm in a gas station or buzzing through an airport, I grab a bag and my day is transformed.

My favorite is the Cool Ranch. Everything from the blue bag, the cool label, and the perfect combination of cool, spicy, and cheesy gets me every time. This past summer my nephew

Ben, a Doritos connoisseur, introduced me to some new flavors that I've been missing. With orange powder around his lips, he introduced me to Poppin' Jalapeño, Spicy Sweet Chili, and something so hot they just call it Blaze. My nephew really likes Jacked, which are ranch-dipped hot wings.

From what I can tell, the Doritos people focus primarily on extreme heat and blowing the top of your head off. I guess, as with any other highly addictive drug, you have to increase the potency to keep them coming back for more. I'm hooked for life.

2. OSCAR PETERSON

A child was born in Montreal in 1925 and his immigrant Indian parents named him Oscar Peterson. At age five he began playing piano under the guidance of his father. He practiced up to six hours a day throughout his childhood and was introduced to jazz and eventually became one of the greatest piano players of all time.

All of this was unknown to me until about five years ago, and now I listen to him every day. I'm listening to him right now and I've never heard anything like him.

He played with Louis Armstrong, Ella Fitzgerald, and Miles Davis. He formed jazz trios with the very best musicians in the world, and always his piano was at the center.

With an ever-present white handkerchief in his pocket, he sat at the piano like it was the only place in the world he was supposed to be. A large, heavyset man with large, powerful, yet feather-like hands, he didn't play the piano as much as become a part of it.

He played with incredible skill and versatility, but more than that he played with his entire being. Everything about the man, about all mankind, came through his music. The hard times, the fun times, the real times. But always tinged with hope and joy that spread across his face and seemed to light up the world whenever he smiled.

His playing elevated his fellow musicians and continues to raise up everyone who listens to it.

And lucky you, you can listen to him right now.

3. BUTTERFINGER

The best candy bar of all time. I'm sure you have your favorite and I'll be happy to hear your case in your book, but on these pages I am allowed and required to crown this perfect nougat-and-chocolate concoction as the undisputed champ.

They're amazing and underrated and now you have a reason to buy one the next time you are staring at that wall of candy under the cash register. A York Peppermint Pattie ain't so bad either.

4. DAIRY QUEEN

There was a Dairy Queen down the road from my high school. It was a freestanding ice-cream stand that looked like something out of a Steven Spielberg version of the 1950s. A giant soft-serve cone outlined in glowing neon lit up the parking lot and put all the customers under a magical glow as they stood in line at the two small windows to place their order.

It seemed like one endless summer night with everyone in the town eventually coming through. Parents trying to keep track of their children in line. Young lovers holding hands, publicly displaying their affection for the first time. Groups of friends, coworkers, and the occasional single adult sneaking themselves a treat on the way home.

And that's the only reason that anyone was there—a treat.

Double swirl cones, sprinkle-covered sundaes, or my favorite, the
Blizzard. The Butterfinger Blizzard. (That's right.) It's soft-serve
vanilla ice cream mixed in a cup with a couple of crumbled-up
Butterfinger bars, so thick that they turn them upside down to
show you how thick they are.

The best part of this memory from my childhood is that I
can still visit it. There are Dairy Queens all around the country
offering the same menu and the same experience that made me
happy when I was young. But returning to the exact one, at the
exact spot, is unparalleled.

Isn't it nice when things last?

5. SUNSETS

You can call me corny, but I don't care, I like a good sunset. That
big fat sun, burning out its last minutes of the day. Humans
walking toward the horizon as if they can pull up a better seat
for this giant orange show.

It's nothing short of a miracle. That this little planet among
billions of stars happens to be just the right amount of distance
from this giant burning star and that we are alive because of
that miracle.

The changing colors of the sky. Twisting purples, screeching
yellows. All burned out and allowing us to go proudly into the
night. It's a goodbye at the end of every day. And we know. Or
we hope. That it will be back to greet us again.

6. THE MOON

And then who shows up? The moon. Another great member of
our team. I love me some moon. Every phase of the moon. The
Cheshire cat sliver, the big fat moon over the ocean on a summer's night when it seems to be closer to us than ever before.

The moon controls us. The moon does stuff to us. It controls the tides, and as we are mostly water, it controls us, too.

All hail the powerful and mighty moon.

When I was in high school, I bought a plastic disk that told you which stars were in the night sky. I kept it in the rusty trunk of my Toyota Corolla in a box filled with stuff that got me out of auto troubles: jumper cables, oil, antifreeze, a wire hanger, WD-40, stuff like that. And stuck in among the oily rags was my star map.

Girls liked when I would take it out and show them some constellation. It was a sign that I was thinking about stuff other than beer, sex, and sports. I did like learning about the stars, but of course a big part of that enjoyment was knowing that I would be sharing it with a beautiful girl.

Some of the constellations are always easy to find. Orion's Belt, the Big and Little Dippers. The North Star is a good one, even though it's all by itself and we mostly lie about where it is. The biggest problem I have continuing this hobby is that I can't see as much as I did before. Not from my eyesight but from how intensely we've lit up the earth. We have so much ground light that we can't see the night sky. Unless we travel farther and farther away from the cities. And that's a good thing.

7. RED WINE

I love wine. I love great wine. Really good wine that elevates the entire room without anyone even knowing why. I know that people like to say there's no difference between cheap and expensive wine, but that's usually said by people who can't afford to buy something nice or become friends with someone who can.

That's not to say that inexpensive wine is bad by any means.

I've had fantastic bottles under twenty dollars and lame bottles made even worse by their high price tag. Taking the time to discover and find what you like is part of the great wine experience.

I will, however, declare that at any price point I drink only red wine. I've had great glasses of white wine and I'm sure I could be convinced otherwise, but with red wine I don't need to be sold. It's deeper, more transformative and soulful.

I like that my doctor told me I should drink it every day. I like that Jesus drank it with his friends. I like that a good bottle can make you travel through space and time. And I also like that it helps make babies.

8. MY IPHONE

Not yours. Not my kids'. Not my wife's. *Mine*. I love it.

I rail against it. I say it's no good. I say that I shouldn't be looking at it too much and that I should lift my head up and look around once in a while, but I will tell you this. I don't want to. I love it too much.

I love when we are alone. My phone comes with me places that even my wife isn't allowed. And it knows way more about me than anybody else. It helps me move around the world. It helps me get fed. It shows me love. It makes me smarter. It does so much. It's everything. Entertainment and sports and work and play. The only thing I can't do is eat it.

But give it time.

9. BURNT PRETZELS

I like pretzels. I like big hot pretzels at the ball game. I like pretzels from a dirty cart on a city street. I'll hold them in my lap and squirt mustard out of packets and risk ruining my shirt. I like pretzels that come in a box that you keep in the freezer. I like pretzel sticks, pretzel rods, and pretzel nubs. I like chocolate-covered pretzels, pretzels dipped in pretty much everything. I really like pretzels.

But the pretzels I love most of all, above all else, in my pretzel parade are burnt pretzels. That's right. Black, burnt-on-the-outside pretzels. They're crunchier than most, salted as any other. I like that they seem to be ruined. They seem like a mistake, beyond pretzel repair, and yet given the chance, you realize they're better than all the rest.

10. REAL BREAD

Not fake bread. Not bread with a zillion ingredients that sits on your shelf for years. Not those hot dog rolls that never gather mold and never seem to be inedible. I mean real, honest-to-goodness bread made out of only four ingredients—flour, water, salt, and yeast. If there are any other ingredients, they better be natural items that add to the flavor, like rosemary, olives, or walnuts.

Bread is good. Bread makes things better. We all need bread. I could live on bread alone. With some cheese.

11. YOU

I've developed a career, a path, and a way of life dependent on other people. Everything funny, crazy, and absurd that informs my work comes from you. All the maddening behavior, inspiring stories, and bizarre occurrences enter my work from watching, listening, and talking to everyone around me.

I've moved around a lot. I've been to more towns than I can remember. But when I am called by a city to return, it is because of the people. And that's why I continue to pack my bags, get on planes, and hit the road. To see you again, hear what you have to say, and try to make sense of it all.

Sure, sometimes you're weird, confused, have crumbs on your shirt, but that's okay. Nobody's perfect. Do the best you can, and if that's not good enough, grab a snack and try something else.

You're doing great. Really.

HAVE YOU EVER FINISHED A BOOK, PUT IT DOWN, AND SAID, "WOW, I *AM* DOING GREAT!" YOU SHOULD.

ACKNOWLEDGMENTS

Writing a book is an isolating endeavor and when it comes time to finally pop my head out of my office with pages in hand I'm lucky enough to be greeted by wonderful people eager to help bring everything into the light.

I would like to thank my editor, Elizabeth Beier, who has been a great guide and trusted friend who often knows what I should write before I do. Rebecca Lang and all my friends at St. Martin's Press, who help spread the word wide and far.

The cast and crew at *Live from Here,* who give me the opportunity to share my writing with a loyal national radio audience. My good pal Joe Rogan, for inviting me in, sharing some bread, and telling the world. Richard Abate, my trusted agent, who thankfully is still laughing along. And the moral support, enthusiasm, and dedication of Josh Pollack, Max Burgos, and Rob Zombie.